T0318403

The Relational Interpretation of Dreams

This book explains the use of dreams as a tool in psychotherapy to provide meaning, establish and maintain a therapeutic relationship, and thus enhance and progress treatment. Maintaining a focus on the synergy between dreams and relationship, it includes interviews with four eminent dream researchers and scholars: John S. Antrobus, G. William Domhoff, Mark J. Blechner, and J. Allan Hobson.

This book explores the synergistic qualities between dreams and relationships, and how that synergy generates biographically, professionally, and psychotherapeutically formative experiences. The book delineates the ways in which dreams provide a foundation for relating, provides a container (Bion, 1967/1993) for the unthought known (Bollas, 1987), creates meaning through relationships, and ultimately fosters dispersion of relational dynamics originating from the culture of the times and more. From a relational psychoanalytic perspective, this book describes the role of dreams in shaping our relational living.

This book provides a unique perspective that illustrates using yourself as a tool in relational establishment, preservation, and knowing. It is ideal for students working toward an understanding of the influence of intersubjective space in clinical interactions and clinicians looking for additional and alternate ways to connect with patients.

Alicia Ann MacDougall, M.S., is an advanced doctoral candidate in Clinical Psychology (Psy.D.) at Antioch University New England. She serves in various roles in national organizations concerned with access to care, leadership, and psychoanalytic theory, practice, and training.

"MacDougall offers us a unique view on dreams positioning interpretation of dreams within intersubjective space where both therapist and patient create meaning of the dream through the intimate connection of the therapeutic relationship. Through her fascinating interviews with prominent dream researchers, MacDougall argues that our dreams are not only past events buried in our unconscious looking for interpretation, but they are invitations to mutual encounters with another. Our dreams, she writes, facilitate relational bonding."

> – **Roy E. Barsness**, Ph.D. is Author of *Core Competencies in Relational Psychoanalysis: A Guide to Practice, Study and Research*, is Founder and Director of the Post-graduate Certificate Program in Relationally-Focused Psychodynamic Therapy and a Professor at the Seattle School of Theology and Psychology

"MacDougall's book brings to life the relational foundation of dreaming, and the importance of a collaborative process and relationship in grappling with the ever elusive meaning of dreams. Through four moving interviews with neuroscientists and psychoanalytic clinicians who are major figures in the area of dream exploration, she portrays a deepening understanding and relationship with her interviewee subjects as they grapple with dreaming, mirroring clinical moments of patients and clinicians together making meaning from dreams."

> – **Arlene (Lu) Steinberg**, PsyD, is co-editor of the book *Sexual Boundary Violations in Psychotherapy: Facing Therapist Indiscretions, Transgressions & Misconduct*, is a Supervisor & Adjunct Faculty member at Ferkauf Graduate School, and an Educational Consultant at Mount Sinai Medical School

"Alicia Ann MacDougall is passionate about dreams and her new book, *The Relational Interpretation of Dreams: When It's About More Than Your Mother*, takes us on an interesting journey about how contemporary master clinicians work with dream material from a relational perspective. Not only will this book be of interest to those therapists seeking a means of deepening their connection to the inner lives of their patients, but also to those with in an interest in the evolution of the theory and technique of dream interpretation as practiced by some of its most artful contemporary practitioners".

> – **Ronald C. Naso**, Ph.D., ABPP, Adjunct Professor, Derner School of Psychology, Adelphi University, Past President, American Board and Academy of Psychoanalysis

The Relational Interpretation of Dreams

When It's About More Than Your Mother

Alicia Ann MacDougall

Routledge
Taylor & Francis Group

LONDON AND NEW YORK

First published 2021
by Routledge
2 Park Square, Milton Park, Abingdon, Oxon OX14 4RN

and by Routledge
605 Third Avenue, New York, NY 10158

Routledge is an imprint of the Taylor & Francis Group, an informa business

© 2021 Alicia Ann MacDougall

British Library Cataloguing-in-Publication Data
A catalogue record for this book is available from the British Library

Library of Congress Cataloging-in-Publication Data
Names: MacDougall, Alicia Ann, author.
Title: The relational interpretation of dreams : when it's about more than
  your mother / Alicia Ann MacDougall.
Description: Abingdon, Oxon ; New York, NY : Routledge, 2021. |
  Includes bibliographical references and index.
Identifiers: LCCN 2020050754 (print) | LCCN 2020050755 (ebook) |
  ISBN 9780367754150 (hardback) | ISBN 9781003162414 (ebook)
Subjects: LCSH: Dreams—Therapeutic use. | Dream interpretation. |
  Cognitive-experiential psychotherapy. | Interpersonal relations.
Classification: LCC RC489.D74 M333 2021 (print) | LCC RC489.D74
  (ebook) | DDC 616.89/14—dc23
LC record available at https://lccn.loc.gov/2020050754
LC ebook record available at https://lccn.loc.gov/2020050755

ISBN: 978-0-367-75415-0 (hbk)
ISBN: 978-0-367-75414-3 (pbk)
ISBN: 978-1-003-16241-4 (ebk)

Typeset in Times New Roman
by Apex CoVantage, LLC

To my sisters, my nephew, my parents, my grandparents, Reet Reet, and Mila and Dusty– the most important relationships in my life.

Contents

Acknowledgments

This book would not have been possible without Theodore Ellenhorn, Ph.D., ABPP.

Ted, your commitment to my success and dedication to ensuring I land on a path that is true to me has led me to where I am – and who I am – today. The lessons you have taught me are invaluable and continue to transform my clinical practice and daily living. *Thank you* is simply not enough to express my gratitude for you and the impact you have had on my life.

To my clients: You have also taught me invaluable lessons, and these lessons have informed the views and line of thinking portrayed in this work. I am eternally grateful for our time together and all I have learned from you.

1 Setting the context
Using dreams to enhance psychotherapy

I had a dream last night. A humorous dream at that. I do not typically dream of my extended family members, but last night, I dreamt of my younger cousin Gregory, whom I feel particularly protective of. Gregory and I were in a local mall together and decided to go into the cafeteria to grab a bite to eat. Upon entering, we came across some of Gregory's classmates with whom he has a tempestuous relationship. I took a step back as I watched Gregory interact with his peers, and, in the blink of an eye (or in this case, the changing of the context of the dream), Gregory was on a miniature red bicycle, fleeing from his classmates who were pursuing him in wooden go-karts. Gregory was frightened, knowing that if his peers caught him, they would beat him up. So, together, Gregory and I ran through the mall – he on his miniature red bicycle and I on foot. To our misfortune, Gregory's peers were gaining on us, and we desperately needed a diversion to slow them down, something to buy Gregory and I some time. As soon as we thought all was lost, my very best friend in this world appeared on an ice-resurfacing machine. My friend wore a bright friendly smile accompanied with warm yet mischievous eyes, knowing that he was about to engage in some drama and save the day. My friend drove the ice resurfacer into the path of the go-karts which gave Gregory and I time to ditch the red bicycle, run out of the exit of the mall, and disappear into the parking lot unscathed.

I woke from my dream and chuckled to myself. I instantly turned over in bed to reach for my phone and message my friend about the dream. We shared a laugh, pondered over the meaning of my friend appearing on an ice-resurfacing machine as neither of us have "ice-legs" or attend sporting events involving skates or an ice resurfacer, and then continued to share our plans for the day ahead.

Any therapist or dream enthusiast reading this book has just formed about 50 different associations to the manifest content of my mind's creation. They have uncovered themes, made interpretations, identified key archetypal images, and more – and that is perfectly reasonable. In fact,

I will admit that I am a bit upset that I am missing out on hearing these insights! However, that is not the point of my sharing this dream. The point lies within the story that the dream facilitates, not the content that the dream possesses. Upon waking, the very first thing I did, even before using the restroom to relieve myself of the bottle of water I had guzzled down the night before, was message my best friend. The relationships I have in my life influenced the dream content, and the dream content influenced my reaching out to relate. Ultimately, the point I mean to make here is to highlight the synergistic quality that exists between relationships and dreams.

Introduction to setting the context

As implied earlier, this book highlights the symbiosis between relationships and dreaming and explicates the various implications of this synergistic phenomenon. The implications discussed throughout this book came to fruition through relating, as I embarked on a journey to interview four eminent researchers and scholars within the field of dreams – pun intended (Gordon, Gordon, & Robinson, 1989). As an organizing framework, I first discuss what research and experts say about the influence of dreams on the relationship within psychotherapy. I then discuss how through a relational psychoanalytic approach to using dreams, therapy sessions can be enhanced as a means to promoting self-growth for clients. To further complicate things, I reflect on the various kinds of relationships people have in their lives and suggest ways in which dreams can be inextricably influential in each of these relationships. Finally, I synthesize the aforementioned topics and the roles they play in fostering formative life experiences and enhancing psychotherapy.

What research and experts say about dreams' influence on psychotherapy

The clinical utility of discussing dreams in therapy sessions has been vastly explored. Research supports that talking about dreams in psychotherapy benefits clients (Schredl, Bohusch, Kahl, Mader, & Somesan, 2000). Cartwright, Tipton, and Wicklund (1980) showed that discussing dreams in therapy has been associated with an increased commitment to therapy. Clients who discuss dreams in therapy report better understandings of interpersonal relationships than those who do not discuss dreams in therapy (Hill et al., 2000), and have an increased willingness to share difficult content (Brink & Allan, 1992; Hill et al., 2013). Brink and Allan found that dreams can serve as an alternative approach to working with difficult populations, while Diemer, Leslie, Vivino, and Hill (1996) found that dream discussion sessions resulted in reduced symptomatology in a distressed adult population. Clients who discuss dreams in therapy share more with their therapists, become more involved in therapy at a faster rate, have higher overall ratings of the psychotherapy process, and are more likely to enjoy the structure of therapy than those who do not discuss dreams (Hill et al., 2000). These clients also report an increased level of depth of therapeutic sessions (Hill, Diemer, Hess, Hillyer, & Seeman, 1993).

While Domhoff (2018) proposes a neurocognitive theory of dreams, he maintains support of the notion that dreams help clients talk about difficult events in psychotherapy. Dreams have the ability to drive conversations, influence topics, and produce movement based off of the essential topics of the internal world (Lippmann, 2000). For a client who cannot actively access internal emotions to drive psychotherapy where it needs to go, accessing dreams may be able to do that for them. As stated by Mark Blechner (2018), "the dream guides its own analysis" (p. 219) and thus tells us what the client needs from us in that moment.

Evidence of the utility of discussing dreams in sessions is abundant. By simply gleaning over the limited review given earlier, it is clear that dreams have an influence on treatment. What all of these studies have in common, however, is a framework that does not pay sufficient attention to the bond between dreaming and relating. While some studies (Hill et al., 2013) examined the impact of dreaming on therapeutic alliance, these studies maintain a lack of appreciation for the symbiosis of dreams and relationships while simultaneously failing to acknowledge the formative experiences fostered through this interdependent phenomenon.

Relational psychoanalytic use of dreams for enhancing therapy and self-growth

To understand the use of dreams via a relational psychoanalytic approach, one must first have an understanding of relational psychoanalytic theory. Relational psychoanalytic psychotherapy, also referred to as relational theory, emphasizes the importance of interpersonal, intrapersonal, and personal relationships (Aron, 1996; Barsness, 2018). Relational theory has its own school of thought and perspective but draws heavily from interpersonal theory, object relations theory, feminist theory, and self-psychology (Barsness, 2018; Benjamin, 1995). Relational theory suggests that humans crave relationships and develop the capacity to relate effectively through a cohesive sense of self (Benjamin, 2010, 2017; Mitchell, 1988). A cohesive sense of self develops via key relationships through processes such as recognition (Benjamin, 1995, 2010, 2017). The process of recognition constitutes that the other in the relationship, such as the mother in a mother–infant relationship, responds to the individual in such a way that confirms for the individual that he revealed an intention, created meaning, and thus has had an impact on the other (Benjamin, 1995, 2010, 2017). In a mother–infant relationship, the responsiveness of the mother to the infant is the basis of the infant's development of his own sense of self and self-agency (Benjamin, 1995, 2017).

Principles of change from a relational psychoanalytic psychotherapy lens are dependent upon the ability to relate intersubjectively (Bromberg, 2008a, 2008b) or to relate through mutual recognition (Benjamin, 1995, 2010, 2017). To relate in this way, however, an individual must have a cohesive sense of self (Benjamin, 1995, 2010, 2017; Mitchell, 1988). Having a cohesive self means the self is not comprised of dissociated self-states (Bromberg, 2012). Instead, a cohesive sense of self is comprised of the integration of self-states, which ultimately makes possible the ability to share subjectivities with another and the ability to participate in reciprocal recognition (Bromberg, 2012).

Distilled to its simplest components, a relational framework posits that the therapeutic relationship serves as a template for the practice and development of relational capacities (Safran, 2002). Through the collaborative exploration of the relational patterns within the therapeutic relationship, the client can develop generalizable skills for managing interpersonal relationships outside of psychotherapy (Safran, 2002). Given this, anything that impacts the relationship in session becomes extremely important to attend to within the therapy hour. While relational theory posits that even negative transferences are important in session, there is strong evidence to support the benefits of a positive transference. The quality of the therapeutic relationship between client and therapist is a key contributor to, and predictor of, favorable treatment prognosis (Ardito & Rabellino, 2011). Client–therapist relationships with stronger alliances have lengthier treatments than those with weaker alliances, and those with weaker alliances are also more prone to therapy drop out (Sharf, Primavera, & Diener, 2010). The therapeutic relationship influences clients' time in treatment, session quality, and overall improvement (Kivlighan, Hill, Gelso, & Baumann, 2016). Given this evidence, we should be paying particularly close attention to factors that enhance the therapeutic relationship. This is where dreams come in (though they were there all along).

Research supports that discussing dreams in psychotherapy increases feelings of connectedness to the therapist (Hill et al., 2013). From a relational psychoanalytic perspective, however, I argue that the key component of dreams enhancing feelings of connectedness lies within the approach utilized for discussing dreams. It is imperative that the dream discussion is a *conversation* between client and therapist, rather than an interpretation. As the therapist and client discuss the dream together in this way, they are participating in a dialogue. The therapist is not superior to the client; rather, the therapist is equal to the client and engaging in a mutual curiosity of the presented dream and its manifest content. By approaching dreams in this fashion, the client becomes an active participant in the process of understanding her internal world more deeply and allows for feelings of connectedness rather than otherness toward the therapist. This form of dream work in psychotherapy sessions is different than other more traditional forms of working with dreams.

Traditional dream work does not employ the client as an active participant in the dream discussion process. For example, in classical psychoanalytic dream interpretation (Freud, 1900/2010), the therapist is the only active participant. After describing the dream, the client takes a passive role for the remainder of the dream interpretation process. The therapist reveals the hidden meanings of different components of the dream, typically without feedback from the client and without providing an opportunity for the client to participate in the construction of meaning of their own internal world (Freud, 1900/2010). The use of dreams from this perspective is concerned with revealing the unconscious content of dreams (Freud, 1900/2010) rather than having a conversation or building a relationship. This type of dream work forces the dreamer into a passive rather than active position, depriving her of the opportunity to be a contributing member to the relationship.

Clients create meaning by being actively involved in the meaning-making process (Mahoney, 1991). Thus, it is important that the use of dreams in psychotherapy is a collaborative experience between client and therapist, rather than a hierarchical representation of an expert therapist constructing interpretations of a client's internal world. As argued by Paul Lipmann, from a relational perspective we do not discuss dreams to look for meaning, rather, we discuss dreams in order to make meaning. It is the role of the therapist, then, to participate in a collaborative process with the client in order to make meaning of the dream (Lippmann, 2000). I propose that in a relational approach to dream work, the client actively participating in the dream discussion enables the development of a positive therapeutic relationship (Safran, 2002). By journeying and considering multiple perspectives together, the client and therapist can increase intersubjective competence or the ability to create a unified experience from two subjective experiences (Benjamin, 2004). Through engaging in mutual dialogue around dreams, the client gets a formative experience for intersubjective relating that then generalizes to relationships outside of the therapeutic encounter (Safran, 2002).

Clients who talk about dreams in therapy have reported gaining insight about their interpersonal relationships (Hill et al., 2000). They have been shown to have enhanced views of self (Mikulincer, Shaver, & Avihou-Kanza, 2011), increased connectedness with emotions (Hill et al., 2013), and improved interpersonal functioning and event insight (Diemer et al., 1996). Due to the synergistic quality between dreams and relationships, clients are able to discuss dreams in therapy while simultaneously building a relationship. In doing so, the client learns how to relate to an *other*, how a respectful other relates to them, and how to exist in a co-created, intersubjective space. These new skills translate well to job searches, academic pursuits, relationship construction and repair, and more. The skills are hard to teach and are, therefore, primarily (and best) learned through experience. Ultimately, these lessons become the foundation for self-promotion – self-growth.

The intimate connection between dreams and different kinds of relationships

There is a plethora of relationships in our lives that we do not think of as relationships. We become so enamored with the obvious types of relating – such as relating with our peers, colleagues, family, friends, teachers, advisors, and even pets – that we do not pay attention to arguably some of the most influential relationships we have. Such connections – our relationship with the culture of the times, our culture in general, society, historical contexts and events, diversity, social justice, therapy, and our careers as a whole rather than those we interact with through our careers – influence us deeply and become integrated into who we are.

From a relational psychoanalytic framework, *every* relationship is an important relationship. Therefore, I would do an injustice to neglect the ways dreams are intimately connected to, formulated because of, and are of interest due to, the relationships we have with these indispensable factors of our being. In the content to follow, I illustrate the inextricable nature of dreams and *all* of our relationships. Whether we like it or not, humans are relational beings and, therefore, have relationships with *everything*.

Summary

In this chapter, I have stated the purpose of this book as being an exploration of the symbiosis between relationships and dreaming. I have addressed arguments made by researchers and experts in the field of dream work that support the use of dreams in psychotherapy. I have provided a relational psychoanalytic framework to using dreams in psychotherapy for enhancing treatment and promoting self-growth of clients. Finally, I have provided an overview of the various forms of relationships that manifest through, with, and because of dreams. In the contents to follow, I refer to the notions presented within this initial chapter. I use these concepts as a framework for illuminating the ways relationships, and consequently multiple lives, are shaped through, within, between, and because of dreams.

2 John S. Antrobus

Keep asking better questions and getting better answers

John S. Antrobus, Ph.D., is a professor emeritus at the City University of New York (CUNY) where he served as Head of the Graduate Program in Cognitive Neuroscience. He received his Bachelor of Arts degree in Psychology at the University of British Columbia in 1954 and his Doctor of Philosophy in Clinical Psychology at Columbia University in 1963. He is a researcher with current interests in brain recognition strategies for information processing and roots in mind-wandering, sleep, and dreaming. He has published extensively on topics including, but not limited to, psychophysiology research on repetition priming, mind-wandering, spontaneous thought and imagery, daydreaming versus perception, neurocognitive perspectives of brain activity during sleep, rapid eye movement (REM) and non-rapid eye movement (NREM) sleep, influential factors of circadian rhythms, and dreaming (Antrobus, n.d.). Information conveyed in the section to follow was generously offered to me by Dr. Antrobus in a virtual interview (which eventually turned into a telephonic interview due to connection problems). In a true supportive professor fashion, Dr. Antrobus agreed to speak with me for this text to assist in my own academic and scholarly pursuits. For this I am sincerely grateful. Thank you, Dr. Antrobus.

Overview of interview

While the interview with Antrobus was initially meant to be a personal account of his work with dreams, I quickly learned how profound the forging quality of research and scientific curiosity is, and how to hyperfocus on one particular subject would be doing a disservice to human sustenance. As stated by Antrobus himself:

> The human mind is probably the most complicated thing there is. Far more complicated than anything in astrophysics. Look, you got 10 to the 11th power neurons, 10 to the 14th power connections are charging.

It's just infinitely complex, and we have to keep looking and asking questions and keep searching. The more we look at more studies, the more exciting it gets frankly – and dreaming is just a small piece of that.

(J. S. Antrobus, personal communication, May 15, 2019)

It was this statement, in fact, that expanded my own views and allowed me to ask better questions regarding the synergistic qualities of dreams.

The beginning of the interview started with an overview of Antrobus's career path. He commented on the accidental quality of his journey, reflecting on the random series of events that led him to where he is today. To explain this venture, Antrobus provided a recap of some history, starting with a mention of Nathaniel Kleitman, Ph.D., a professor at the University of Chicago. He reported that Kleitman worked in a group at Chicago University and eventually published on the discovery of REM sleep (Aserinsky & Kleitman, 1953). Post-discovery of REM sleep, a student from Chicago University named William C. Dement completed his dissertation, which provided dream work findings aligned with publications by the Kleitman Group (J. S. Antrobus, personal communication, May 15, 2019). After completing his training in Chicago, Dement accepted a job at Mount Sinai Hospital in New York to work with Charles Fisher, a psychoanalyst who was actively studying dreams in relation to schizophrenia and sleep deprivation. During this time, Antrobus had been attending Columbia University in pursuit of his Ph.D. through Antrobus's doctoral program, William Dement was invited as a guest speaker to present on his work with dreams. Antrobus's first wife was very interested in dreams at the time, and so he and his wife (through exposure to Dement at his guest lecture) became involved with Dement's work on dreams.

Eventually, in pursuit of a faculty position, Dement moved to Berkeley, California, ultimately leaving his lab in New York to Antrobus. Though Antrobus did not have any personal interest in dreaming, it was his fascination with the ability to look at, and detect things going on in, the brain that kept him involved in the field.

While all this was happening, Antrobus did not lose track of his interest in what was then termed "mind-wandering" and is now termed "spontaneous thought and imagery." In the early stages of his graduate education, he was robbed of money he had set aside for graduate school, forcing him to get a job to compensate for the loss of funds. This is when he began to work in a lab at Columbia with Jerome Singer who had just gotten a research grant to study mind-wandering. Together, Singer and Antrobus started the field of mind-wandering. Initially, the field was not picked up by many, which allowed Antrobus to step aside from that field for a bit and focus on dreaming and sleep research in the interim. Eventually, with the development of the ability to image the pre-frontal cortex, the field of mind-wandering grew and ultimately became the field of spontaneous thought and imagery – a field that Antrobus remains intrigued by, still.

After providing me with this recount of historical events in his life's journey, Antrobus explained, with enthusiasm, instruments he developed to explore mind-wandering in laboratory settings. He described how these activities led to a science interested in the "how and why" of brain activity, and how those questions influenced research around the world. With a follow-up question about the influence of others' research on Antrobus's theories, we found ourselves in a conversation concerning J. Allan Hobson's theory regarding random activity in the brain stem (Hobson & McCarley, 1977). Initially, Antrobus found himself thrown by Hobson's theory, yet in hindsight he took a critical stance on the theory, suggesting that discovering a random activity just means you have not yet found what that activity is functionally related to. This stance on Hobson's theory then led Antrobus to report on a paper he wrote (1983), concerned with REM sleep in the earlier versus later part of the night. The mention of this paper became a frameshifting topic, which facilitated the evolution of an eye-opening conversation.

Through my own curiosity, I asked Antrobus for his current views on his REM sleep theory. He paused for a minute and then continued to explain that he did not entirely know. He commented on the nature of studying such a phenomenon and how the work is particularly hard to orchestrate. His remaining thoughts on this stance were rendered as follows, "I've been one of the most agnostic of all the people on the function of dreaming and its theoretical basis because people jump to believe something because it's there, but they don't test those ideas very well" (J. S. Antrobus, personal communication, May 15, 2019). Antrobus then continued to discuss a multitude of disciplines that widely professed theories despite a lack of data. He took a disapproving stance on classical psychoanalysis, dating his thoughts all the way back to Freud as he suggested that Freud's followers did the opposite of what he had suggested. According to Antrobus, Freud was an incredible revolutionary who insisted that good theories serve as the basis for better theories. Though Antrobus agreed with this statement, he commented on the tendency of psychoanalysis as a field to maintain Freud's original philosophies and form an orienting approach around them – something Antrobus coined as a belief system rather than a theory. He then continued to support Freud's notion saying, "A theory is a basis to represent what you know now, in order for you to ask questions to make the theory better," reinforcing this with the stance that a good theory should change every 3 to 4 months. Antrobus then used this delineation of thought processes to reinforce his original answer to my question, explaining that this area of research is hard to test and that after losing his sleep lab and moving to CUNY he has not been following the area of dream research. Put simply, he would not formulate a decisive stance in the absence of decisive evidence.

In listening to Antrobus's story, I went through a whole day's worth of internal responses in the matter of 2 minutes. Identifying as having a psychoanalytic theoretical orientation, I of course felt defensive of my home theory with thoughts racing through my head like, "That was over 100 years ago!, There is plenty of evidence supporting this theory now!", and "Why does everyone hate on psychoanalysis so much?" Then, my graduate-student thoughts came racing in, "Maybe I don't know as much as I think I do, maybe the data I know of is wrong. Maybe I didn't read the articles closely enough." Those were soon flooded with thoughts birthed by my innate drives to relate to another human being, "Hey! You are conducting an interview, snap out of it and just listen!" So, I did. I listened and then did what every normal human being with innate drives does – I let my defenses get the best of me and tried to bring the conversation back to dreams. Who would have thought?

In my feeble attempt to pull the conversation back to dreams (while simultaneously integrating topics touched upon by Antrobus to maintain connectedness), I asked, "Despite the lack of evidence of so much when it comes to dreams, and despite the limitations of researching dreams, I wonder if you have a view on dreams and their meaningfulness, or if you view them as meaningful or not, despite the lack of evidence" (I threw that last "despite the lack of evidence" in there for good measure). At first, Antrobus asked me to clarify what I meant by the word *meaning*. Then, he commented on the abstract quality of the question. He followed this comment with facts we know about the relationship between humans and earth and how he believes that relationship is then allied with sleep (i.e., earth rotates about every 24 hours and there is no need for all species to be competent the full 24 hours – particularly at night for non-nocturnal species and so, there is sleep – to put it simply). After discussing the rotation of the earth, he then mentioned brain metabolism and the increased activity of the brain in the last 2 hours of REM in comparison to the first 2 hours of REM. He reported that this shows the brain is preparing for the waking state and that this was particularly interesting to him. Antrobus then shifted his focus to psychotherapy and again to psychoanalysis (perhaps my defenses failed me) stating that psychoanalysis makes the mistake of believing dreams will tell you something you would not come to in another way. Antrobus elaborated on this comment by saying:

This is not a repressive society we are in today, not like Vienna in the 1880s – 1890s. We don't need to go back to dreams to find out some feeling you are not aware of. I don't think at least, not nearly like you did back in those days of mass suppression of spontaneous thoughts . . . I think it was very useful in the 1890s, but I don't think it's so useful today. I think you have to pay attention to other kinds of things.

Antrobus was right. The last sentence of this statement was the wrecking ball through my own defensive process, allowing me to open my eyes and truly appreciate the anomaly unfolding in front of me (well, through my ears via telephone). My relationship with dreams was impacting my ability to relate to Antrobus. I was having a hard time asking questions and navigating the conversation. What I had to realize, however, was that I was not in Vienna in the 1890s or that I was not in the context I thought I would be in. I was in a conversation with a brilliant scientist, who has a deep appreciation for testable hypotheses that work toward achieving a scientific truth (a temporary truth until we find a better one at least). I was out of relationship with what was happening in that moment, in the here-and-now of experiencing, and resultantly was having a hard time learning through connection as I typically do. I needed to pay attention to other kinds of things – the things relevant to the context that I was in.

Upon having the epiphany – or, defense mechanism talking to, as I like to call it – I started asking questions relevant to the context of being in conversation with a scientist interested in spontaneous thought and mind-wandering. I asked questions specific to mind-wandering and received answers that truly enriched my learning. Both Antrobus and I became more engaged in the conversation. We were able to have a true back and forth. I revealed questions and uncertainties I held about the field, and they were met with answers supported by facts and evidence. When I posed a theory, I was reminded that beliefs prevent people from asking questions. "It is important that people can ask questions and have doubt, and that is one of the most important values that I have actually," Antrobus shared, and I recognized that this approach was exactly what allowed us to have an active and engaged conversation rather than a bland "ask question–give answer" interaction. By casting aside my belief system regarding dreams, I was able to ask Antrobus questions and be curious about the information he was relaying to me. By asking questions and having doubt, I was able to engage in a relationship. To my surprise, this approach actually led us back to dreams. Antrobus spoke to the depressing quality of the limitations to the National Institute of Mental Health (NIMH)-funded research. NIMH primarily funds research that is specifically related to some type of therapy, leaving little, if any, funding for curiosity and exploration of questions, ideas, and theories. Additionally, there has been a decrease in funding for professor and graduate student research, making it even harder to ask intellectual questions and investigate theories and doubts. Dreams, unfortunately, are a part of this debacle.

As the interview went on, I continued to ask questions directly related to the context. I heard of Antrobus's most recent area of interest, and as my investment in his stories grew, relating became more palpable in our conversation. Antrobus explained how dreams (something he knows I am interested in) are in fact a piece of the bigger issue he is currently concerned with. He then began to ask about my own interests within and in addition to dreams. I explained my proclivity toward dreams and brain-injuries and was met with wise words:

> The main thing is to have a passionate interest like you have and follow up and see where it takes you. One of the pieces is to avoid beliefs of any sort. All of your understanding is conditional on the information we have today. All of our knowledge is only partial. It's an approximation to better ideas, and that's what we have to realize. We need to keep asking better questions and getting better answers so we can ask the better questions.

Now each day, I keep asking better questions.

Analysis of interview

In a relational psychoanalytic approach to psychotherapy, the therapeutic relationship is used as a vessel for change. Growth happens through the relationship via introspection and interaction in the context of what is happening in the here-and-now of the relationship – in the intersubjective space. This is exactly what happened for me during this interview. When I first began the interview, I had a specific agenda in mind. I had a list of questions regarding dreams that I wanted to ask Antrobus and was looking for specific answers. As the interview continued, I learned that I was not going to get the answers I was looking for. Antrobus had shifted away from his original line of research and had a critical view of psychoanalytic theory as a whole. Upon this realization, I became defensive. I attempted to shift the conversation back toward dreams to fill my own agenda and was not being attentive to the here-and-now of the intersubjective space. It was not until Antrobus had pointed out the necessity of paying attention to other kinds of *things* was I able to re-engage in a productive way. As a therapist in sessions, I am often paying attention to other kinds of things – those things being my reactions to my clients and their reactions to me. By paying attention to visceral reactions, words, facial expressions, body language, and more, I am able to better understand what is happening in the moment. I then bring that realization into the intersubjective space to facilitate healing through the reintegration of whatever was not being attended to in that moment. Consequently, when Antrobus made this comment, I connected to it immediately, thus realizing that I had been reacting rather than relating and therefore not being mindful of what was present in the intersubjective space.

Antrobus started his career during a time where psychoanalytic theory had really not been tested very well. There was a superfluity of treatment approaches for the psychologically ill that were premised from 100+ year-old theories with little empirical data backing the claims. Being a scientist, Antrobus developed a critical and disproving relationship to this type of practice, as he understood the value of empirically derived evidence and testable hypotheses. He maintained this association throughout the growth of his career, so much so, that it had permeated the intersubjective space of our interaction. I, on the other hand, started my career during a time of evidence-based psychoanalytic treatment. In my time, studies had yielded significant effect sizes for the efficacy of this approach (Shedler, 2010). I respectively developed my own relationship with psychoanalytic theory – one so favorable that I had deemed this philosophy as my primary treatment model. Given this, it makes sense that I became reactive toward Antrobus's claims on psychoanalysis. Though, it was not until Antrobus highlighted the essentiality of looking at other "things" that I realized the magnitude to which both mine and Antrobus's relationships (such as our relationships to the culture of the times, and our generational differences) were influencing the way we were relating.

With this awareness, I began to understand the conversation within the context of the intersubjective space. I took the here-and-now of that co-created territory into consideration and asked questions that reflected a recognition of this arena. Questions were rooted from an understanding of who I was conversing with – a cognitive, neuroscientific researcher who deeply appreciates facts and evidence and has a critical relationship with a historically (but no longer)

ill-researched theory. In shifting my mindset and taking the relationships of the other into consideration, room was created for curiosity and exploration. Rather than be persistently asked questions regarding an area of work that he has been disconnected with for quite some time, Antrobus was able to speak about his passions and become interested in my sentiments as well. He asked what enthralled me and on sharing I received invaluable advice in return. I was growing through the intersubjective space of the relationship we had established.

The conversation between Antrobus and I provided me with a formative experience. Through taking a relational psychoanalytic stance on our interaction, I was able to look inward and appreciate the intersubjective space that manifested from a difference of contexts that, for me, was initially challenging. Antrobus and I each had a different relationship to dreams. Once I became cognizant of the influence of this difference, I was able to appreciate the here-and-now experiencing of the interface and integrate valuable information from it into my personal ethos. Rather than *dreaming* about my pre-determined – and therefore learning-limited – agenda, I was able to engage in recognition (Benjamin, 1995) which facilitated betterment for all involved.

Independent of our interviewer–interviewee dyad, the conversation between Antrobus and I revealed additional formative experiences. Through relationships, Antrobus was introduced to dream work, and through dream work, Antrobus became engaged in more relationships. It was through his story of his previous work as a dream researcher that the synergistic quality between relationships and dreams became strikingly apparent.

Antrobus's first wife was especially interested in dreams. Due to their shared interest, she and Antrobus attended a guest lecture on dreams. Antrobus's relationship with his wife and her relationship with dreams swayed them to approach the guest lecturer and facilitate a relationship with him. Through this relationship, she and Antrobus became involved in sleep and dream research and eventually inherited a sleep lab. Numerous publications on sleep and dreams resulted from this inheritance, ultimately contributing to the field as a whole, and establishing relationships with others in the field. As mentioned in his interview, Antrobus discussed the work of J. Allan Hobson and his colleague McCarley (1977). He discussed the impact of Hobson and McCarley's work on his own views of dreams as well as Hobson's impact on others in the field. Likewise, he commented on tensions this created within the land of dream research, as there appeared to be some for, and some against, Hobson's theories. While the superficial understanding of this story line is glaringly obvious – Antrobus was recounting history – a comprehensive consideration includes an observation of the nature of the relationships formed through dreams. Through being interested in, and working with dreams, professionals developed relationships between colleagues and within self-perspectives. Fundamentally, a synergistic event, the symbiosis of dreams and relationships, acted as a catalyst to the commencement of professional identity.

Summary

In this chapter, I provided an introduction of cognitive neuroscience researcher John S. Antrobus, Ph.D. I narrated an interview conducted with him in which we discussed dreams, mind-wandering, sleep research, and the importance of continually asking questions. He taught me that a good theory is the stepping stone for a better theory, and while the intricacies of a particular phenomenon may be of interest (such as dreaming), hyperfocusing and refraining from asking different types of questions deprives one of receiving better answers. I provided an analysis of our interaction to explicate the ways in which various types of relationships (i.e., our relationships to the culture of the times) influence our relationships to other people. Finally, I provided a description of the formative experiences brought about by the synergistic quality of relationships and dreams.

3 G. William Domhoff
Sharing information

G. William Domhoff is Distinguished Professor Emeritus at the University of California, Santa Cruz (UCSC). He has held several positions at UCSC including, but not limited to, acting dean for the Division of Social Sciences and chair of faculty. After his retirement, he continued to teach courses, conduct research, and write for publications. He is a researcher concerned with power from a sociological perspective, as well as a front-runner in empirical dream research. He has over 40 publications spanning more than seven decades on the scientific study of dreams, including four books and multiple collaborative works in academic journals. Topics range from content analysis of dreams (Domhoff & Kamiya, 1964) to neuroscientific underpinnings of dreaming phenomenon, including consideration of the relationship between dreams and the default network (Domhoff & Fox, 2015). Domhoff received his Doctor of Philosophy in Psychology (Ph.D.) at the University of Miami in 1962 (Schneider & Domhoff, 2020), where he was influenced by, and worked closely with, dream researcher Calvin Hall.

The following sections of this chapter contain information shared with me by Dr. Domhoff through a telephonic interview. Dr. Domhoff graciously agreed to communicate with me and, upon meeting, generously devoted multiple hours to our conversation. He shared a wealth of information and has therefore contributed greatly to the contents of this book. For this, I earnestly thank you, Dr. Domhoff.

Overview of interview

It seems to be a developing theme of this book that I did not anticipate interviews to evolve as they did. Domhoff's interview was no exception. Domhoff and I spoke about plenty of dreams, dream research, his view of dreams, and his path to becoming a pioneer of the scientific study of dreams. What stood out most throughout our conversation was Domhoff's propensity for relationship, and how this propensity was inextricable from dreams.

To begin our interview, I asked Domhoff if he would share with me his journey of becoming a dream researcher. He agreed good-naturedly and began to discuss his interests as a graduate student. He was intrigued by human motivation, the human psyche, personality, and the *why* and *how* of what people do what they do (see, think, move, etc.). His undergraduate program, however, required numerous behaviorist courses and valued the use of animal models for scientific study. Domhoff quickly learned he had no interest in animal research so, after his undergraduate training, he continued to a Master of Arts degree program where he worked closely with a humanistic psychologist. He later pursued a doctoral degree in psychology at the University of Miami – a new program self-identified as humanistic. It was here that Domhoff met, and began working with, dream researcher Calvin Hall. Around the same time Domhoff and Hall began working together, William C. Dement was publishing articles on a sleep cycle called rapid eye movement (REM) sleep and non-rapid eye movement (Non-REM) sleep (Dement & Wolpert, 1958). Coming from a rigorous psychology graduate program, Domhoff valued quantitative research. What Dement's findings then allowed for was an integration of rigorous quantitative study with Domhoff's new collaborative work on the study of dreams. As stated by Domhoff, "Now, what this meant, and I used to say, it suddenly moved dreams from the periphery – from the fringe, from the same level of respect that parapsychology has in psychology – right to the center of things." He then continued that Calvin Hall had a system to classify and quantify dream content. This system eventually found its way into Domhoff's dissertation (1969).

> It gave me an idea of the whole thing, but also a certain defensiveness and defiance towards the . . . you know . . . established ways of doing things in psychology. My dissertation was called – and it's almost like in your face – *A Quantitative Study of Dream Content Using an Objective Indicator of Dreaming.* Put that in your pipe and smoke it!

(It was at this exact moment that I decided "this guy is awesome.")

Subsequently, Domhoff's dissertation design was used for a larger study – a grant for which was awarded to Calvin Hall. By the time this grant work was underway, Domhoff had already moved to California. So, Hall hired someone to conduct this work while Domhoff contributed from afar. Through a collective team effort, the journal article, "Problems in Dream Content Study with Objective Indicators: I. A Comparison of Home and Laboratory Dream Reports" (Domhoff & Kamiya, 1964), was published.

At the time of these publications, Domhoff noted that people began to shift away from interests in dreams. He attributed this to preconceived notions of dreams containing elaborate symbolism (as portrayed by Freudian, Jungian, and Noe-Freudian practices) not being supported by dream research. This evoked curiosity in Domhoff and Hall, as they too had expected to find more symbolism, such as sexuality in dream content. Resultantly, Domhoff and Hall worked together to create a measure that could assess for symbolism in dreams. The measure evaluated what Domhoff and Hall termed *Unusual Elements*. In an initial study, little unusual elements were found in dreams. Then, a re-study yielded a mere 10% of lab samples containing unusual elements (as cited in Domhoff, 2018). The elements embodied little sexuality, more aggression than anticipated, and no significant evidence of symbolism in dreams. This was enough to convince Domhoff that dreams were a mundane event. The mundane quality of dreams, however, held more weight than expected. In our conversation, Domhoff made note of the hopefulness elicited by dreams for the treatment of the mentally ill. In the nineteenth century, philosophers made a connection between dreams and psychosis, which gave the illusion of understanding dreams as being a way of treating psychiatric patients. When studies on dreaming became possible, however (particularly after Dement's papers on REM sleep), it became more apparent that dreams held no promise for the mentally ill. "The important point is, that dreams were being a disappointment to treatment," as stated by Domhoff. This gave even more reason for people to move away from dream research.

While studies revealing the lack of utility of dreams as a treatment approach were being conducted and published, Domhoff was teaching at California State University, Los Angeles. Courses included introduction to psychology, child psychology, personality psychology, and social psychology. Being the early 1960s, these courses occurred in the middle of the Civil Rights Movement. Students were attending demonstrations at Berkeley and were riled up by what was called the Free Speech Movement. This energy, in conjunction with teaching and thus learning an abundance of human psychology, drew Domhoff into political sociology research. It was during this phase, Domhoff admitted, that he too became one of the many who left dream research in pursuit of other ventures.

Calvin Hall never left dreams, but when he finished his research in Miami he decided he had enough of Florida and wanted to return to California. Once in California, Domhoff and his family would often visit "Uncle Calvin," and Hall would update Domhoff on the happenings of dream research. Though Domhoff had maintained his work in sociology and power, he continued to be, in effect, mentored by Calvin Hall. Despite no longer being involved in dream research, Domhoff continued to teach a course on dreams into the early 1980s. Students in this course often asked about the Senoi dream theory, and having no knowledge of this theory, Domhoff brought it to Hall. Hall shared what information he knew of the theory, and then Domhoff did research on his own. Upon further exploration, Domhoff discovered that this theory had no pragmatic grounds. This inspired Domhoff (1985) to write his book, *The Mystique of Dreaming: The Search for Utopia Through Senoi Dream Theory*. The book was mainly about the sociology of ideas, but dreams were a main contributing factor of its contents. After writing this book, a former co-worker of Hall's (Robert Van de Castle) invited Domhoff to speak at the Meeting of the Association for the Study of Dreams. This allowed Domhoff to make people aware of his book, and ultimately brought him back into the world of dream research.

Though this story has an abundance of influential factors, the common thread that kept Domhoff in touch with the dream world was relationships. As stated by Domhoff, "How did I remain in dreams? Because Calvin Hall was in Santa Cruz." Additional circumstances that continued to influence Domhoff's work included an early retirement opportunity in 1994 with full support from the university he was working for at the time (University of California Santa Cruz – he began working here in 1965 as founding faculty, shortly before Calvin Hall moved to Santa Cruz in spring of 1966). Having University support post-retirement, he was able to spend his time continuing to conduct dream research with small faculty grants. He spoke of a "dream team" full of students who worked for him on dream studies. He spoke highly of this team, commenting on the closeness of the group. He reported that when the informal leader of the team became gravely ill, it "took the heart right out of the work," and the team dismantled despite the leader recovering from their illness. The thought of losing a member was devastating and changed the nature of the relationships within the group, as well as the group's relationship to the work. If one member was not there, no one else felt they could be there. Domhoff (2002) dedicated his book, *The Scientific Study of Dreams: Neural Networks, Cognitive Development and Content Analysis*, to this "dream team."

Despite this hardship, Domhoff's position as an early retiree gave space for continued research pursuits. He commented on his ability to spend a month or two on dreams, and a month or two on power, while still maintaining teaching some classes. Retirement brought a lot of free time due to a lighter responsibility load, affording space to pursue interests and publish findings.

While personal relationships proved to be extremely influential in Domhoff's career, relationships with the work of others in the field upheld their own significance. Domhoff reported being particularly influenced by David Foulkes, who in 1982 published a book on dreaming in children. His book claimed that children do not dream before the age of 5. Domhoff was skeptical at first, but after many conversations with Hall and investigating follow-up studies of this claim, as well as reanalyzing dream reports from Foulkes, Hollifield, Sullivan, Bradley, and Terry's (1990) cross-sectional study – the results of which are published in Domhoff's (1996) book *Finding Meaning in Dreams* – Domhoff became convinced that there is a developmental factor to dreaming. These findings went against a lot of existing theories, so, not many in the field believed this claim – including Allan Hobson.

Domhoff commented on his frustrations with Hobson for rejecting this theory even into the year 2000 where he claimed that he had no doubt that even neonates dream. He also commented on Hobson's beliefs that Domhoff's work regarding the content of dreams was trivial. Hobson believed that people were inhibited in the lab, but Domhoff was confident in the methodological soundness of his studies and baffled by Hobson's rejections. Domhoff also commented on the likelihood of more physiologically minded individuals to deny Foulkes's findings. The denial of Foulkes's data proved to be a strong talking point in our conversation, as it was brought up multiple times – particularly within the context of ignoring information. Domhoff spoke about the value of sharing information for the greater good, rather than denying information that is available or standing behind a theory that is contradictory to existing data. He reflected that he is now critical of individuals who practice in this way. The stance that he used to take was, "Oh! I've got some data for you guys!", and he would like to see more of that attitude practiced within the field. Ultimately, Domhoff valued collective efforts in pursuing greater knowledge – something that was truly encapsulated by his following statement:

> I guess it is really right to say that I really have been influenced by a great many people and what I read. In other words, I'm not sort of an independent thinker or independent researcher that relies on only what I research or what I think. I'm always trying to assimilate what other peoples' research is trying to piece together. I have more fun sort of synthesizing, and I do like other people's new findings. I read new findings, and that I really do enjoy. So, I am influenced by other people. I was influenced by meeting Calvin Hall. I was influenced by the fact that he lived here from '65 to '85. I was also influenced by the Civil Rights Movement, by the anti-war movement, and by my students.

His stance was revealed not only in words, but in his conversation with me as well. Domhoff maintained an informative stance throughout our discussion, providing me with over 3 hours of data, facts, and recollections of research and empirical evidence. He shared his own work, the work of others (e.g., Mark Solms, Tony Zadra, Mark Blagrove, John Antrobus, Bart

Sanders, Jessica Andrews-Hall, and Kieran Fox, as well as all mentioned earlier), and relevant historical contexts to the world of dream research. The one thing I was certain of after this interview was that Domhoff had taken a mentoring stance, a stance of sharing information as a means of helping me pursue my own work with dreams in an informed and assimilated fashion.

After recounting his own personal history, Domhoff and I got to talking about dreams in general and our thoughts, feelings, and relationships to dreams as a whole. Knowing that I am in a Psy.D. (Doctor of Psychology) program, Domhoff turned the conversation toward uses of dreams in psychotherapy. In his view (as in mine as well), the dream is an avenue for expressing things that are too difficult to just say directly. Domhoff shared:

> the dream becomes an occasion for people that aren't good at talking or comfortable with talking about, themselves, to indirectly start talking about themselves . . . I don't for a minute because of my theory, think that dreams are not valuable for therapy.

Domhoff then continued to speak of the great difficulty of using dreams in the culture of the times we are in currently. He commented on the pressure from health insurance companies to see results in treatment after an allotted amount of sessions and how this restricts room to discuss dreams in therapy.

For a closing question, I asked Domhoff about his views on the culture of dreaming. From here, we got into a conversation of how dreams *are* a culture. They give us a belief system and we construct meaning around them. Given the culture of the times we are in, our beliefs of what dreams are changed, and Domhoff again relayed how his beliefs of what dreams are have changed multiple times throughout the years as new information regarding dreams and how to study them became available. He then shared a quite impactful comment with me, "So I think meaning keeps getting reconstructed, and that makes it fun. That makes it an adventure for me and that's why, you know, I think I'm still going." Domhoff was referring to fun, to play – an inherently relational phenomenon. Research is a field of play – a field of excitement, adventure, and discovery. It is a field of back and forth sharing of information among colleagues. It is the revitalization of the fundamentals of developing relationships (Winnicott, 1971/1991) – and dreams have been vital in this game for Domhoff and many more.

Analysis of interview

Domhoff's career and professional identity were built first and foremost through relationships. As stated by Domhoff, he does not view himself as an independent researcher or thinker – he is greatly influenced by those he has relationships with, as well as things he develops relationships with, such as new research findings and books. To separate Domhoff from his relationships in considering the development of his professional life would be to discount the key and foundational components of how he got to where he is today. His relationship with Calvin Hall influenced him tremendously and is what first introduced him to the world of dream research, and eventually brought him back to it after having left for a while. Even for work unrelated to dreams, Domhoff's relationships to others, such as his students, were influential in his alternate professional pursuits.

In addition to relationships forming his professional identity, Domhoff's professional interests, particularly his interest in dreams, brought additional relationships into his life. Domhoff, looking for research assistants to help conduct and manage his dream research, hired a group of individuals who became the "dream team." The dream team members were inseparable, and when a forced separation occurred due to illness, the team dismantled. The bonds manifested through working with dreams had become so strong that it was intolerable to work in the absence of any of the members. As stated by Domhoff,

> It just destroyed us. The thought that this person might die was so unbelievably heavy for all of us. . . . Those were the glory days, but they got personal. . . . we might have done another year and other really interesting things, but it just took the heart right out of it. It almost felt wrong picking up the work . . . you know, it just didn't feel right.

The indivisible nature of relationships forming through dreams was echoed through the inseparability of the connection between the members of the dream team. The *Field of Dreams* (Gordon, Gordon, & Robinson, 1989) was all about relationships as well, was it not?

Multiple other relationships were established in Domhoff's life through dreams, particularly in the professional domain. Throughout our interview, Domhoff mentioned and referenced over ten professionals who have contributed to his own views of dreams, and whom he has influenced as well. Domhoff spoke of frustrations with others in the field, such as Hobson, for denying data from the work of colleagues such as Foulkes. Hobson's relationship to Foulkes, therefore, influenced Domhoff's relationship to Hobson – and the infrastructure of each of these relationships is dreams. In Domhoff's (2018) latest book, *The Emergence of Dreaming*, he has a dedication to Foulkes, which comments on their friendship – yet another relationship forged by our minds' nightly creations. At times throughout our interview, Domhoff also mentioned of mind-wandering research in its relation to dreaming – a field co-established by the interviewee in the previous chapter, John S. Antrobus.

In addition to his relationships with people, relationships to other factors have also been influential in Domhoff's personal and professional life. Domhoff's relationship to the culture of the times has been a formative component to his identity. Dement publishing on REM and non-REM sleep provided opportunity for Domhoff to pursue quantitative dream research with Hall. The lack of evidence of symbolism in dreams at a time where dreams were a hopeful answer to the treatment of the severely and persistently mentally ill initiated a movement away from dream research, which Domhoff followed. Teaching during the Civil Rights Movement peaked Domhoff's curiosity in the sociology of power. Though unrelated to dreams, this interest was a result of what was happening in society around him at that time. While teaching in the 1980s, a popular dream theory of the times (the Senoi dream theory) facilitated conversations within established relationships and eventually brought Domhoff back to dream work. As time progressed and neuroscientific research became more abundant, Domhoff's beliefs in dreams changed with each new, relevant, discovery. All of the above examples are evidence that Domhoff's relationship to the culture of the times he is, and was in, served as a formative experience in his professional identity. Interestingly enough, Domhoff even commented on the ways in which the culture of the times is influential to formative experiences of others as well. He discussed the restrictions implemented by health insurance companies in the world today, and how this greatly impacts the type of psychological treatment received by patients – any clinician, student, or aspiring professional reading this book surely understands the formative aspects of psychological treatment.

What struck me most about Domhoff was his readiness and desire to share information. He is a characteristically relational individual, and this is evident by the trajectory of his career. As he shared with me, Domhoff enjoys dream research because meaning keeps getting reconstructed as new findings emerge. This gives him a sense of excitement and adventure in his work, and ultimately highlights the relational quality of research – a field of collective discovery and adventure, full of collaborative efforts and, most importantly, play (there is a reason why mad scientist kits are so popular among kiddos these days). Meaning-making does not happen solely through the data. Meaning-making in research happens through the relationships formed that make the gathering, assimilating, analyzing, interpreting, and sharing of data possible.

The relationships Domhoff has had through dreams have shaped his life and, consequently, are shaping the lives of others. His research has served as the basis for works of other professionals and has fashioned relationships between people who may have otherwise never met. In his life, dreams have provided a foundation for relating, and reciprocally, relating has provided a basis for exploring dreams. His relationships to the culture of the times, to others, and to his own work have shaped his interactions with, and connections to, colleagues and aspiring graduate students like myself. From a relational psychoanalytic perspective, dreams have established the intersubjective space between Domhoff and many with whom he interacts, thus further highlighting the synergistic quality of relationships and dreams.

Summary

This chapter began with an introduction of dream researcher G. William Domhoff. I provided a review of our telephonic interview in which we discussed Domhoff's professional journey. We spoke of formative relationships in his life, as well as professional endeavors that produced relationships. Domhoff shared information and relayed the importance of distributing and assimilating evidence and data. He described key historical events and the influence of these events on his professional identity. I then provided an analysis of key components of our interview, including the relational quality of conducting research, an overview of key constructive relationships and events, and lastly, the indissoluble nature of relationships and dreams in both Domhoff's life and the lives of those he has influenced.

4   Mark J. Blechner

Having the privilege of entering the lives of others

Mark J. Blechner, Ph.D., is a psychoanalyst psychologist who practices in New York City. He received his Bachelor of Arts from the University of Chicago and his Doctor of Philosophy in Clinical Psychology from Yale University. He was awarded his certificate in psychoanalysis from the William Alanson White Institute of Psychiatry, Psychoanalysis & Psychology, where he currently trains and supervises psychoanalysts. Dr. Blechner is a clinician with interests in dreams, sexuality, and psychoanalytically oriented approaches to working with acquired immunodeficiency syndrome (AIDS) patients. He has taught at renowned institutions such as Columbia University, Yale University, and New York University. He served as Editor-in-Chief of the journal *Contemporary Psychoanalysis* and was the Founder and Director of the human immunodeficiency virus (HIV) Clinical Service at the White Institute. He has written extensively on topics such as neuropsychoanalysis, psychopathology, gender and sexuality, AIDS and HIV, experimental psychology, psychoanalysis, and dreams. Dr. Blechner has published many articles and book chapters as well as four books which examine societal reactions to human sexuality, the efficacy of psychodynamic and psychoanalytic approaches to working with HIV and AIDS patients, and dreams (Blechner, 2020).

The remainder of this chapter is a narrative of material shared with me by Dr. Blechner via virtual interview. Dr. Blechner responded to my interview request immediately and graciously offered to speak with me. He was the first of my series of interviews reported in this book; admittedly, I was nervous to meet with him. As our virtual meeting developed, however, Blechner acquainted me with his clinical and relational style – a warm, friendly, and welcoming demeanor with a deep curiosity of the *how and why* of interpersonal interactions. Throughout our conversation, I found myself intellectually enthused and relationally jubilant (ok, so I have a bias with my psychoanalytic leaning and all – but I will further discuss the implications of this bias later). Dr. Blechner spoke with me for nearly 2 hours and provided not only answers to my questions, but also eye-opening world-views of the inherently relational constituents of dreams in psychotherapy, as well as clinical practice as a whole. I am deeply appreciative of your shared wisdom, your openness, and your time, Dr. Blechner.

Overview of interview

My interview with Blechner began with a setting-of-context. He asked where I was located geographically and I gladly shared this information, as well as some additional facts like where I am from originally. A typical conversation starter at first glance, this setting-of-context holds significant foreshadowing to the importance of the consideration of contexts within the remainder of our dialogue. Acknowledgment of geographic, familial, theoretical, academic, cultural, and relational contexts – particularly with consideration of their affiliations to dreams and dreaming – was actually what allowed Blechner and I to connect in the way that we did.

After I shared a bit about myself, I asked Blechner about the *how* and *why* of his journey to working with dreams. Blechner began his story with recollections of an assigned summer reading in high school. He was instructed to read Freud's *Introductory Lectures on Psychoanalysis* (1917/2019), about a third of which is devoted to dreams. At the age of 15, Blechner was captivated by Freud's theories and began to write down every dream he remembered. When he went to for his undergraduate education at the University of Chicago, he became aware of the university's graduate-level courses on dream interpretation taught by Erika Fromm. Blechner approached Fromm, asking to take part in her courses, and after much deliberation she eventually agreed. While taking these courses, Blechner heard of the sleep lab of Allan Rechtschaffen – a dream researcher from the same university. He decided to pursue work in this laboratory so he could assimilate his knowledge from his own ideas of dreaming (amplified by courses with Fromm) with physiological dream research. Though only working in this lab for a short period of time, Blechner got to know a lot of people through this position and commented on the interconnectedness between lab and university staff (i.e., Fromm served on the dissertation committee of a graduate student working in the lab). After graduating from the University of Chicago, Blechner continued his graduate-level training at Yale university where he pursued his Ph.D. in clinical psychology. There was not much work being conducted on dreams while Blechner was at Yale, but he was able to work with a number of psychoanalysts during this time, which allowed him to refine his own ideas about dreams. Then for his predoctoral internship, Blechner worked at the Psychiatric Institute of Columbia University College of Physicians and Surgeons. While interning, Blechner's patients repeatedly brought dreams into session. He commented on the nature of the dream sharing, and how the dreams often told him something about the patient that he or she had not. For Blechner, what this meant was that dreams were important not just because Freud said so, but because there was clinical utility in discussing them with patients. The dreams did not just fulfill his own interests, but they truly helped his clinical work as well – particularly his large caseload of individuals diagnosed with psychosis or Borderline Personality Disorder.

In 1977, Blechner started his own private practice. Influenced by his experiences at Columbia, he worked a great deal with dreams, practicing a lot with his own approach to the masterpieces of our sleeping states. Basically, the manifest content provided Blechner with clues to experiences patients have had in waking life. It was at this juncture in our interview that Blechner began to share stories of the ways in which dreams have helped his clinical sessions. For Blechner, dreams have provided insight to the past experiences of patients, have served as an opening to begin treatment, and have also reflected an outlet for anxious distress so that therapeutic work could be pursued. The more Blechner spoke, the more excited I became, as these dream stories were quite similar to experiences I have had in both my clinical practice and my own life. As Blechner continued, I followed his storyline with enthusiasm, itching to hear what came next. He continued to tell me that despite using his own theories to work with and conceptualize dreams, he sometimes found himself at a loss regarding the directionality of these discussions. Then, in 1979, he started his analytic training at the William Alanson White Institute, and his understanding of dreams was expanded once again.

While at William Alanson White Institute, Blechner had two courses on dream interpretation. One was taught by Leopold Caligor and the other by Paul Lippmann. During one of these classes, Blechner mentioned in passing that he had been observing changes in the dreams of his borderline patients. A member of his class overheard this discussion and encouraged Blechner to write his observations. The encouraging comment materialized as Blechner's (1983) first psychoanalytic paper called "Changes in the Dreams of Borderline Patients." It was this publication that propelled his dreaming career.

Once published, Blechner became known as someone who worked with dreams. He began teaching dream courses to analytic candidates and became involved with the Association for the Study of Dreaming, an international group concerned with all schools of dream interpretation and biological research. At one gathering in Oahu, Hawaii, Blechner attended a dream group that utilized the Montague Ullman approach to working with dreams. Blechner was amazed. He approached the instructor at the closing of the group, who informed him of training weekends held in the Westchester

County of New York. Upon his return from Hawaii, Blechner found his way to Ardsley, New York, to attend one of these weekend workshops. He recounted the workshops as extraordinary, explaining that from the moment you got there on Friday, you analyzed dreams until the minute you left on Sunday. In this one weekend, Blechner learned a whole new approach to working with dreams. This newly acquired knowledge vastly changed his approach to working with dreams and became integrated not only into his clinical work but also into his teaching.

Though colleagues were skeptical of the openness of psychoanalytic candidates in sharing their dreams in this Ullman style group, Blechner decided to try anyway. When no one volunteered to share a dream in the first group, Blechner opted to share his own, and once realizing how the process unfolds, all candidates wanted to share their own dreams. The dream groups became a favorite component of Blechner's courses and were so successful that Blechner decided to begin running dream groups aside from his courses. To date, he has one dream group that has been running for 14 years and another that has been running for 12.

While the Ullman-style dream groups had launched a plethora of dream-focused activities, as well as a new founded approach to using dreams clinically, the dream groups provided Blechner with something more as well. As reported by Blechner, sharing his own dreams in these groups had sensitized him to the intense anxiety associated with, and elicited by, sharing intimate information for interpretation. The experience of sharing his own dreams afforded an understanding that had not previously existed – an understanding that would ultimately help him relate to patients in a way that "doesn't take over the process, but expands the process," as stated by Blechner himself. Blechner's understanding of this intense anxiety influenced a non-conventional approach to treatment. He realized that patients, particularly borderline patients, would often turn the conversation onto Blechner and away from themselves. Instead of interpreting their redirection, Blechner followed their lead, which ultimately aided in working through therapeutic impasses, as the increased vulnerability from Blechner allowed patients to work through their own vulnerabilities and identify with aspects of Blechner's (1992) own self-reflections. Eventually, Blechner began to use this approach with dreams as well, where insights regarding his own countertransference were attained through associations to patients' shared dreams.

Blechner (2001) continued to experiment with techniques for working with dreams within his therapy sessions, some of which debuted in his book, *The Dream Frontier*. This work was then followed by the publication of his second book, *The Mindbrain and Dreams: An Exploration of Dreaming, Thinking, and Artistic Creation* (Blechner, 2018), in which Blechner wrote of his own theory of dreams. The influence behind his hypothesis in his second book, however, goes far beyond his own clinical practice. To explain this, Blechner began to discuss the works of Mark Solms and Jaak Panksepp in the field of neuropsychoanalysis. Being highly interested in the intersection of neurology and psychoanalysis since his graduate training, Blechner went to meetings held by Solms and Panksepp, a high percentage of which were concerned with dreams and dream processes. A contributing factor to this focus on dreams, as reported by Blechner, was due to the work of J. Allan Hobson (Hobson & McCarley, 1977), who published a paper discounting Freud's philosophy of dreams, claiming that dreams were random activity from a very old part of the brain, the pons, which was then translated into a story by the cortex. Blechner commented on a 25-year feud between the two scientists and conveyed the findings of Solms which showed that people with damage to the pons still dreamt, providing evidence against Hobson's theory. Despite this feud and back and forth of research, Blechner shared his stance of agreement with Hobson's claims that Freud's idea of dreams disguising information was probably not true. This agreement, in addition to evidence from Solms, was incorporated into Blechner's new conceptualization of dreams which was then professed through his second book.

At this point in the interview, Blechner had shared the timeline of events that led him to the present day. I was fascinated by his story, and, being a *bit* of a theory nerd, I was deeply curious of the ways in which I could integrate my own knowledge of psychoanalytic theory with Blechner's wisdom about dreams. To do this, I decided to share my own associations to his story. I wondered about the link between beta and alpha elements of language (Bion, 1967/1993) and manifest dream content and waited for Blechner's response. It was in this moment, the moment of my exposing my theoretical context, that our conversation truly evolved.

Blechner responded with enthusiasm to my inquiry. He shared his own thoughts on the implications of language on the manifest dream content and tied these thoughts back to theories reported through some of his previous publications. I reacted to this answer with additional questions grounded in theoretical readings, such as Christopher Bollas (1987), in which something interesting began to transpire. Blechner began to share a story from a study group in 1967, The Kris Study Group at the New York Psychoanalytic Institute, which Blechner reported as having a negative impact on psychoanalysis with their findings (or lack thereof) of no special material derived from dreams. Blechner then commented on his own training at the William Alanson White Institute and how this training was more concerned with dreams than most classical Freudian approaches – something he believes to be deeply influenced by the information from The Kris Study Group. In hindsight, I recognize this moment as a moment of vulnerability on behalf of Blechner. After sharing my own theoretical context, Blechner shared a story of how psychoanalytic theory, particularly as it pertains to dreams, became discredited. It was as if he had shown me a hesitation on his end to speak of theory initially (as he had spoken mainly of facts until this point, such as timeline of events and different publications) which was then freed up by my own vulnerability in sharing my theoretical context (something that I in fact did not do in other interviews discussed throughout this book). It was at this point that a relational phenomenon began to transpire.

We continued to discuss the theoretical underpinnings of particularly favorable dream approaches. We spoke of the recognition processes (Benjamin, 1995) manifested through the Ullman-style groups, as well as Ferenczi's idea of the necessity of discovering things about yourself through working with patients in order to help the patient (Aron & Harris, 1993). We spoke of Carl Jung and the importance of understanding his theories in order to comprehend dream work, as well as the significance of Jung's easy-going approach to clinical practice – including his sharing of his own dreams with patients to promote equality, and thus comfort, and increased associations within sessions.

Already on the topic of sharing therapist dreams, I asked Blechner about his own dreams, and how, if at all, they have helped maintained his interest in dreams throughout all these years. He paused for a moment and then began to reflect on early childhood during which he had a repetitive dream. He reiterated his original statement of Freud inspiring his interest in dreams as a theoretical subject matter but credited his reoccurring childhood dream as the pivotal event in his deep-rooted interests. From here, Blechner and I began to discuss the dreams of children, and he shared stories from his own family of origin in which children's dreams reflected sophisticated symbolism (these dreams did not contain words, but only images and emotion). I then recalled my own childhood experiences of dreams, and how these inspired my interest in dream work. I view dreams as an extension of play – the kind of play that does not require words but, instead, representation of experiences through imagery. Dreams deeply influence the way I view the world. I asked Blechner if he had a similar experience, and he began to speak of the differences between himself and others in this regard. He spoke of our westernized culture, and how, in general, our culture does not speak of dreams as much as others. He was reminded of a woman from one of his dream study groups who was from Jamaica. She once shared with the group that a family morning ritual would be to share a dream at breakfast if you had one that you remembered. The dreams would be interpreted by the grandmother, and the interpretations were important to the family as a whole, regardless of who had the dream.

Our discussions on culture continued, evolving to considerations of the intersection of different cultures with dream interpretation, eventually leading us to a conversation regarding the intersubjective space of the patient and therapist and the influence of this space on dream work. Many of the questions raised between us remained unanswered, consequently prompting us to reflect on the puzzling aspects of dreams. We spoke of the ambiguity of dreams, the mysteries of repression (i.e., patients writing down dreams and then denying the dream happened until being reacquainted with their dream journal entry), and the inevitability of shame as well as the difficulties of proving shames' existence.

Blechner and I did not stop at shame (I guess you could say we were shameless in our sharing of thoughts). We spoke further on topics such as dreams and trauma; who is more likely to find utility in working with dreams, and who is less likely to do so; as well as the reasons supporting these differences. Our dialogue transformed from being fact oriented to intriguing curiosity. We even progressed to play as we joked and laughed together toward the end of the interview. In response to a humorous story I shared, prefaced by personal motivations for pursuing work with dreams, Blechner replied with a remarkable perception of the significance of dream utility:

> You could say maybe that is the original motivation, but after a while it starts to develop all this kind of intellectual fascination and also you start to feel like, "Well, it's not just about me. I have the privilege of entering peoples' lives," and really you could still say maybe it helps me understand myself, but it really does help other people. It is an amazingly wonderful feeling when you can do that.

He was right. Through dreams we relate, and through relating we enter and shape lives. While our various contexts set the frame of the ways in which these relationships unfold, the dream is a common denominator, and, in its absence, the relationship may have never existed – such as my own relationship with Dr. Blechner.

Analysis of interview

Blechner was trained as an interpersonalist. This theoretical leaning was clear throughout our conversation; however, it is difficult to decipher whether the training influenced the person or the person influenced the understanding of the training. Given that this is a relational book, I am opting for the latter of the two. This is particularly because I truly do not believe that Blechner would have had the same conversation if someone other than myself had been conducting the interview with him. The intersubjective space of Alicia MacDougall and Mark Blechner was entirely co-created. Take for instance, the beginning of the interview in comparison to the end of the interview. At first, Blechner and I were concrete and fact oriented in our interaction. I asked questions that were pre-prepared and written down in front of me, and he answered through delineating a timeline of events. Toward the end of the conversation, though, we were engaged in a mutual dialogue full of curiosity as well as give and take. This happened first and foremost through mutual contributions to the relationship, particularly as it pertained to the various contexts associated with dreams.

In my experience, during the beginning of the interview, Blechner had not quite figured me out yet. He was not sure of the *context* from which I was coming. Without knowing my context, Blechner was speaking into a void, unsure of if he was providing information for ridicule, praise, or for translation into hard data. As far as he knew, he had signed a consent form and therefore the *how and why* of our interaction was something like – *participation in study via interview for data gathering on working with dreams*. In my mind, however, the conversation was more than that. In order to let Blechner know this, it felt important to share more about my context. This insight was materialized through recognizing that context was important to him when he asked about my geographical location at the onset of the interview.

As soon as I began to show vulnerability and disclose aspects of my contexts, the conversation between us became more free-flowing. I shared my theoretical orientation (my theoretical context), and this set a new frame for our conversation – one in which Blechner knew he was not speaking with someone who would discredit the seemingly ambiguous nature of analytic concepts (notice I used the word *seemingly*). At the beginning of the interview, he knew I was a New Englander who frequented New York, which set the premise for acknowledgment of a particular culture that exists both in working and living in this general region of the states. My academic context was set in multiple ways. When I first reached out to Blechner, I stated my academic standing. Then, at two different points in our interview, I mentioned my status as a student, once in a comment reflecting my respect for the work of those more experienced than me, as well as during the sharing of a fond memory I had of an undergraduate professor, thus showing that I greatly value my academic advisors and the wisdom they bestow. Familial and relational contexts were also shared as Blechner discussed dreams of family members. This gave me a window into his family life. At another point during the interview I had said to Blechner, "For me, part of why I've become increasingly interested in dreams is because of the way it allows for connections to develop between two people," which explained my relational context as being the importance of connection – not acquisition of data. In sharing all of this with Blechner, the *how and why* of our interaction shifted from participation in study via interview for data gathering on working with dreams, to graduate students interested in knowing how dreams create relationships and wanting to learn through experience via connecting with an expert in the field. This new understanding of the "how and why" of our dialogue then set the framework for the remainder of our conversation.

The more Blechner and I shared our contexts, the more engaged in the conversation we became. Understood from a relational standpoint, we were bringing fuller versions of ourselves into our dialogues and relating to each other in a more integrated manner (anyone who was once a student can understand the difficulty in conversing with an individual who only presents one aspect of themselves – such as a teacher who is only presents as a teacher and shows no sign of humanity while abiding by this stringent, role-abiding guideline). While discussing dreams, we disclosed a significant amount of context. Once these contexts were mutually identified, they served as a container (Bion, 1967/1993) for our conversation. A conversation that was both linguistic and pre-linguistic, as we found ourselves contemplating the non-contemplatable and trying to express the inexpressible, deeply imbedded in the un-thought known (Bollas, 1987) of experiencing. Through each of us contributing to the relationship, we were able to communicate safely and comfortably – as evidenced by the presence of play and curiosity in our interchange. With dreams as the basis, an entire relational phenomenon ripe with vulnerability, connectedness, and co-created inter-subjective experiencing was able to transpire.

Aside from the relationship established between Blechner and myself, Blechner spoke of relationships that were formative in his own career – a lengthy list: (a) His high school teacher who assigned him Freud as a summer reading sparked his interest in dreams as theoretical construct; (b) Erika Fromm provided insight into dream interpretation; (c) working in the sleep lab with Allan Rechtschaffen provided the opportunity to integrate physiological dream research with theories learned in Fromm's classes; (d) courses taught by Leopold Caligor and Paul Lippmann further enhanced his knowledge of dreams; (e) connections to classmates within dream courses influenced the start-up of his publishing career (ideas which first and foremost originated from therapeutic relationships and conversations with patients); (f) his interactions with the instructor of his first ever Montague Ulman style dream group led him to the weekend workshop on the Montague Ulman dream groups which he then incorporated into his books and used in courses he instructed to share with developing analysts; (g) his interactions with Mark Solms and Jaak Panksepp connected him to the world of neuropsychoanalysis, as well as the works of fellow dream colleagues such as Allan Hobson, whose work greatly influenced his own theory of dreams; and (h) finally, his relationship to his family members also contributed to his personal theory of dreaming, particularly with respect to symbolism. Throughout Blechner's professional development, dreams provided a foundation for relating, and relationships were also foundational to thoughts regarding dreams. The two were, and are, indissoluble.

Every aforementioned relationship contributed significantly to Blechner's work. In return, his professional life is now shaping the lives of others. He publishes written work to support current and developing clinicians, supervises analysts in training, works clinically with patients, and even consults with non-psychologist authors who are interested in dreams. Through dreams, Blechner enters others' lives and finds meaning. Whether it be through a psychotherapeutic interpretation or engaging with a graduate student in an inspiring conversation – perhaps the dream is really the royal road to the relationship.

Summary

This chapter provided a professional development timeline of Mark J. Blechner, a psychologist and psychoanalyst who works clinically with dreams, teaches courses about them, and has published extensively on them. The contents shared before contain a report of a virtual interview conducted with Blechner. Topics discussed include work with patients, work with colleagues, and the significance of dreams in providing an opportunity for deep connection and understanding. Blechner reported on formative events and experiences within his own career and proposed questions that could shape the careers of others. An analysis of this interview included a relational psychoanalytic understanding of the interactional style between interviewer and interviewee, as well as the formative elements of this particular interface. A consideration of containing experiences that prompted this relational phenomenon was cited. Finally, the chapter provided a written image of the lives Blechner has touched through his work with dreams.

5 J. Allan Hobson

Recognizing the person behind the scientific discovery

J. Allan Hobson, M.D., is a psychiatrist and Professor Emeritus at Harvard Medical School in the Department of Psychiatry. In 1933, he attained his Bachelor of Arts degree from Wesleyan University. He later obtained his medical degree (M.D.) in 1959 from Harvard Medical School. For his medical internship, he worked at Bellevue Hospital in New York and then later became a resident in psychiatry at Massachusetts Mental Health Center. Dr. Hobson has held numerous prestigious positions including serving as a clinical scientist at the National Institute of Mental Health, as well as holding the title of Special Fellow in the Department of Physiology of the National Institute of Mental Health at the University of Lyon, France. He has received numerous awards, including the Peter Farrell Prize from the Division of Sleep Medicine, Harvard Medical School; Distinguished Scientist Award of the Sleep Research Society; and the Benjamin Rush Gold Medal for Best Scientific Exhibit, American Psychiatric Association. He has been inducted as Honorary Member of the American Psychiatric Association, as well as the Boylston Medical Society. He has contributed to, and participated on, countless editorial boards for medical journals as well as served roles in national and regional medical committees. He has functioned as a consultant and educator through his work as a professor and researcher and even through local communities by extending invitations to his Dream Museum (Zezima, 2007). He has 20 book publications on dreams in which he is the author, co-author, or co-editor. He has written an incalculable number of monographs, medical text-book chapters, and scientific journal articles. He is a researcher with interests in the history of neurology and psychiatry, the neurophysiology of behavior, and sleep and dreaming. He has dedicated a lifetime to work in dream research at Harvard Medical School (Hobson, 2015).

On May 13th, 2019, I visited Dr. Hobson at his home in Vermont for an in-person interview. Our conversation quickly shifted from a strictly academic exchange to a dialogue influenced by a deep interest and curiosity in the person behind the research. From the moment we first spoke, I was acquainted with Hobson's pervasive and infectious scientific curiosity. After spending half of a day together, I had developed a deep appreciation for the mind of a genius. All that follows in this chapter is derived from the conversations between Hobson and me on that brisk New England spring day. My visit with Hobson was nothing short of awe-inspiring. Dr. Hobson, I cannot express enough appreciation to you for opening your home and sharing your time and elements of your world with me. Our interaction has greatly shaped my outlook on the humanity in science as well as the intricacies of personhood. Thank you,

Dr. Hobson.

Overview of interview

Dr. J. Allan Hobson is highly misunderstood. He has been deemed inflexible for standing behind the activation–synthesis theory of dreaming (Hobson & McCarley, 1977), despite competing hypotheses. Though a perceivably rigid comportment, the rigidity truly resides in holding onto misunderstandings of this hypothesis. Colleagues within the world of dream research view Hobson and McCarley's theory as a testament to the meaninglessness of dreams. Hobson, however, in his interview with me as well as in his book, *Psychodynamic Neurology* (2015), testified to the inaccuracy of this accusation. As stated by Hobson (2015):

> I have denied this meaningless charge by saying that meaning is revealed by dreams, not concealed as Freud and his followers asserted. I have denied the exclusive reliance on physiology by stating, loudly and clearly, that I am not a reductionist and that I am not an eliminative materialist. I think that psychology and physiology are both indispensable and sadly admit that they are all too rarely given the equal plate that I accord them.
>
> (p. 197)

What is reflected in this statement is something that I picked up on rather quickly in our interview. Throughout our time together, it often felt as though I was the one being interviewed. Hobson asked me questions regarding my personal motivations for speaking with him, as well as pursuing study within the field of dreams, reasoning for my choice of education endeavors, and even my family-of-origin dynamics. He is a man who questions *everything*. His motivations for doing this are alluded to in his statement given just before this paragraph. Hobson is a true polymath, his unyielding pursuit of knowledge providing him with endless data to assimilate and incorporate into his interpersonal interactions, worldviews, and scientific and clinical inquiries, theories, and conceptualizations.

If working with dreams was like working in digital photography, researchers would focus on the pixels, while clinicians would focus on the gestalt. Hobson, however, seems to be a rare exemplar of the necessary integration of these two mindsets. As our interview demonstrates, Hobson's worldview exposes the limitations of Cartesian disintegration. Hobson's pursuit of truth and lack of allegiance to any one methodology or theoretical stance is a mystifying and easily misunderstood way of being for those holding a discipline-aligned epistemology. His approach is ripe for *othering*, from a relational standpoint, as his thinking defies categorization. I view his critical eye and eschewing banner waving for one theory or another as essential for the advocacy of personifying the humanity influencing our work.

When I emailed Hobson asking for an interview, he replied rather quickly, requesting a phone conversation for additional inquiry before coming to a decision. So, we set a time for a couple weeks out. When I called Hobson, I was not at all prepared. Not because I am an unprepared person, but because I had prepared for a quick overview of my goals for our interview and not a game of rapid-fire, with half-second answer allotment and 84 questions. In the matter of 7 minutes, Hobson knew where I grew up, where I live now, why I wanted to write about dreams, where I go to school, how many satellite locations my school has and in what states, my estimated timeline of completion for this project, my future career endeavors, my previous clinical training, others I reached out to for an interview, my theoretical orientation, the clinical demographic I work with most, and my opinion of the weather in Northern Vermont in May. The man does not waste time.

About a month later, I was on my way to Northern Vermont to visit Hobson at his home. My trip promised an interview, a visit to his dream museum, and even some lunch. When I arrived, I entered his home and sat on the opposite side of his desk from him. Behind me were hundreds of journals, which I would later discover were all of Hobson's self-recorded dreams. I began the interview by asking Hobson how he got interested in dreams. He shared his story of going to medical school with aspirations of becoming a surgeon. He quickly realized that he hated surgery though and shifted his goal to psychiatry – a suitable endeavor given his bachelor's thesis on Freud and Dostoyevsky. He was interested in Freud and believed he wanted to become a psychoanalyst. In his second year of medical school, however, he had a professor who was fiercely anti-psychoanalytic. This professor, a cardiologist, had a wife with schizophrenia. This man's life experiences in conjunction with his anti-psychoanalytic demeanor contributed to Hobson's growing interest in the neurobiology of mental illness and disenchantment with psychoanalysis. Hobson went onto a residency position at the National

Institute of Health (NIH), where he was hired to work with participants in schizophrenia research. It was in the ward at NIH that Hobson met Fred Snider, a researcher studying sleep. Hobson began working with Snider and after some time decided he wanted to study sleep more extensively. This is when he began working with Edward Evarts, a neuroscientist examining the neurobiology of sleep. Hobson attributed this position to the catapulting event of his career. In addition to these events, Hobson made mention of two important discoveries that occurred in the year 1953. He recalled the discovery of REM sleep (Aserinsky & Kleitman, 1953), as well as the discovery of the double helix model of deoxyribose nucleic acid (Watson & Crick, 1953). These two discoveries were the groundwork for what Hobson considers to be the continuing expansion of science.

I asked Hobson if it were not for these experiences if he would still be in dream research. He paused and said "I will answer that in a different way." From there, he commented on the importance of endless curiosity and a continual search for something that makes you happy, much like his own quest that brought him from schizophrenia to dream research. He referenced Freud saying:

> Like Freud always said, he was an adventurer, and I think that's true. He was an adventurer, and what you have to be is something like an adventurer. You keep looking until you find something that really makes sense to you. I kept moving until I found something that I wanted and made sense to me.

This exchange was yet another glimpse of the magnitude of his scientific curiosity. Hobson never stops searching.

In light of this, we began to speak of the ways in which Hobson's own dreams have changed throughout the years. This is when Hobson directed my attention to his journals. To date, he has been working with dreams for over 50 years. He explained to me that he is more mindful of his dreams now than he once was and that he records his dreams every single day. He shared that his own dreams have changed throughout the years for reasons he believes to be due to age and as a function of looking at them. He made his position known that he values dreams for psychiatry and psychotherapy, and that he also values them as a tool for ourselves for self-analysis and self-understanding. From here, our conversation shifted from interview to a relational dialogue. He asked me about my own dreams, curious if I was a vivid dreamer. Since my vivid dreams were a huge motivating factor for these interviews, I gladly shared that I frequently have vibrant and extremely detailed dreams. He asked that I reach for a journal behind me and open it up. His journals had not only dreams, but also pictures of his children, places, objects, and important memories from his life. He told me about one of his sons, whose baby footprint was inside the cover of the journal I had chosen, and then reached for the journal so he could read me an entry. He read through half of one dream, then flipped to a different page and began reading another. I smiled as I listened, fascinated that I was hearing the dreams of Allan Hobson.

Hobson finished the second dream and then looked at me and said, "So let me take a break there and ask you a question. Do you have a brain?" I was not quite sure where he was going with this, so I said, "I'd like to think so." "You know so. It is a fact that you have a brain," he said. "Yes," I replied. "But you don't think about it or think of you having a brain? You think about having a mind." I nodded in agreement. Hobson then continued:

> In your mind, I say, is a brain function. So, when you think about your mind you are thinking about your brain. Why don't we think about our brains? Why is it so uncommon to have anyone tell you ever that they have a brain when it is so obvious that it must be the case?

Hobson's inclination to question everything was rearing its head here. "I mean, the first thing that comes to *mind*," I said, "is how it feels cultural to me almost. I don't know, I almost feel like for some reason, and this might be my own culture." Hobson interrupted before I could continue, "See now I think, excuse me, but I think that the answer is reasonable, but I think it's wrong. It appears cultural, but it is probably biological. What might it be if it were biological?" I oddly felt tossed back into elementary school, the exact moment being when I was handed a subtraction test with 100 problems on it that I was expected to solve in 60 seconds. (Math is not a strong suit of mine, so I typically would just stare at the page for a minute or do a few problems and then start crying.) I shook my head and brought myself back into the here-and-now. "Why is he asking me this? What does he want to know? What is he trying to find out?" I asked myself in my head. "I guess I won't find out unless I just go with it," I found myself thinking. So, I paused, searched my brain for a minute, and then replied, "Hmm . . . if it were biological, I don't know . . . I am trying to think in terms of evolution," "Yes! Do that!" Hobson exclaimed. "And uh," I continued, "Why would it be evolutionarily beneficial to think of having a mind but not having a brain?" "Yes, go ahead. That's a good question," said Hobson. "I'm not sure, um," I paused again. "What are the possible explanations?" Hobson asked. "Well," I began, "some kind of protective factor, um, I don't know what the protective factor would be, but I am also thinking something to do with reproduction, and I am trying to think about innate, primitive urges humans have naturally and how that could be connected to." "Well, nobody knows the answer," interrupted Hobson. "But, it is a good thing to put on your application for a job – that you are interested in finding out more about why people are so unaware of having a brain." You know that look you give when you just did something really embarrassing and you cannot believe yourself? Yes, that is the look that was on my face in this moment. I was running on half of a cup of coffee and a bite of a granola bar after having woken up at 5 a.m. to get ready and get on the road for the 3-hour drive up to Hobson's place to be there by nine in the morning – I sat in front of him with the little hamsters in my head running on their exercise wheels on overdrive trying to find an answer to this question, and there is no actual answer. Ha!

Hobson then shared his own thoughts about this question. He provided a profound theory of the evolutionary components of our lack of acknowledgement of having a brain in regards to an ingrained blissful ignorance and then stated:

> It is a very extraordinary fact that we are unaware. As we think of ourselves, we think of ourselves as an *I. I* is a person. We think of that in psychological terms and that is a great weakness of psychology. We are fooled into thinking that we are only minds.

Of course! I thought to myself, then began a dialogue of all of the biological components of our personhood that we know for a fact that we have but do not think of as having, such as genes. Why, however, could I not think of this prior to Hobson's prompting? I am currently in a Psy.D. program and I am being trained first and foremost as a clinician, and my overarching worldview is compatible with that of my discipline-aligned epistemology. I think primarily in terms of human psychology, the gestalt of the photograph (I mean, look at the material in this book). Contemplating big picture questions from a solely psychological epistemology though (like I first attempted when I brought up culture) does not quite cut it because the thinking and any answer that derives from it become a bit too isolated. Hobson, however, is a polymath. When he thinks and conceptualizes he does this from the framework of multiple epistemologies simultaneously (in the example just given he was considering both biological and psychological epistemologies and emphasized the downfall of considering a large question from an either–or stance rather than a both–and stance). Hobson's multifaceted intellect penetrates each interaction he has.

From a relational standpoint (yes, psychological epistemology I know – but you chose to read a relational psychoanalytic theory book), Hobson was gauging my ability to think from more than one epistemology. He already knew what I was being trained in but wanted to see if that was the only mindset I was willing to, or capable of, working from. He was assessing the intersubjective space, attempting to determine in what way he could or would relate with me. Hobson finds it important to think from multiple perspectives and becomes quite abrasive in his interactions if he feels the other is not willing to do this. For example, in his book *Psychodynamic Neurology*, he speaks pointedly of his disagreements with Mark Solms. He states that Solms does not accept his neurobiological discoveries and, thus, is not truly integrating phenomenological psychology with neurobiology (Hobson, 2015). Bringing this back to the above dialogue with me, my answers and reactions to Hobson became a critical indicator of the relationship that was about to unfold. He began to share his own dreams and some of his own life story with me and then stopped in the middle of this to assess my intellectual leanings – to assess what he could and could not share with me. Had I answered his question by saying, "This is a purely psychological phenomenon," my guess is that he would have thrown a plethora of neurobiology facts at me, insisting that I take these facts into consideration and refusing to engage with me further until I did. If I had completely shut down and said, "I can't answer that," he would have perceived that as my having a lack of scientific curiosity and would have persistently asked additional questions until I began to show signs of curiosity. Or, he would have just skipped that altogether and made an attempt at persuading my views to align with his own (more on this later). Instead, however, I entertained his question. I alluded to my own scientific curiosity by posing questions as I searched for an answer. While I thought primarily from my own epistemological framework, I was able to shift sets and integrate multiple frameworks when prompted by Hobson's response – I showed that I was teachable. When I learned a bit from Hobson, I considered neurobiology, psychology, genetics, and more, and revealed my own assimilating processes as I verbally exposed my existing knowledge and my curiosity of the unknown. By doing this, Hobson realized that he did not need to take his typical uncompromising defensive stance with me as he has with so many others as seen throughout this book (he is a man who defends his work and beliefs). He recognized that I was willing to learn from him, and not excessively defend my own knowledge. I was willing to be open to multiple perspectives. In Hobson's newly acquired understanding of the potential space (Winnicott, 1971/1991), our conversation began to transform.

As soon as we began discussing genetics, Hobson asked about the hereditary history of my own family. This inevitably led to a conversation about my mother, who had a massive and debilitating stroke at the age of 41, when I was just 21 years old. As time passed, disclosures became deeper. I shared my becoming head of household for my three younger sisters, disabled mother, and foreign-tongued illiterate grandmother. I discussed financial hardships and challenging family-of-origin dynamics that exacerbated the complexity of our situation. Given that I am an Italian-American, Italy naturally came into the conversation. Hobson shared his own associations with Italy, a country he is particularly fond of as he is married to an Italian native and spends half of the year living in Italy. I shared that I want to take my mom to Italy one day, and Hobson spoke of the importance of travel with family. He reflected on his own traveling, most of which he did alone. He remembered wanting to be in solitude for these trips, but in hindsight expressed regret in not traveling with family more. Hobson then shared a story of William James, informing me that James was educated at home and abroad by his father. He used this story as an illustration to his point: "When you have children you want to spend time with them. You want to take them on trips." He then asked if it would be possible for my mother to fly. After explaining that I would need clearance from her neurologist, Hobson gave some suggestions of how to approach this and also rattled off some names of neurologists he knew who could help if clearance was not granted. After this exchange of information, Hobson interposed, "Where should we go from here?" It is my natural tendency to go with the flow so I let the contents of our previous conversation pave the way as I shared an observation of the ways that my mother's dreams have changed since her stroke. With this, Hobson asked of my knowledge of Mark Solms' work. I admitted I had some but not a lot of awareness of his work, and he shared conclusions made by Solms (1997) that he agrees with – that the integrity of the temporal–parietal junction and frontal lobes of the brain impacts dreaming. As an addendum, Hobson also shared a follow-up research question in regards to Solms' work. He suggested that if I put on my predoctoral internship applications that I found a way to conduct these studies then large research universities like Yale University would find me particularly appealing. He then began to consider my family-of-origin dynamic as he remembered that I play a vital role in the management of life for my family. He concurred that being closer to home in Connecticut would make things easier for them and myself. He started to name other places in Connecticut that I could apply to for my internship and also named a few places in New York within commuting distance, considerations that would only be taken by a mensch.

Hobson told me that he believes his acceptance to Harvard Medical School was based on the recognition of his curiosity. He shared his belief that renowned institutions would be interested in me if I portrayed the same curiosity. From here, he also said that he was trying to sell me on the idea of making journals. I shared that it would not take much convincing because dream journals are already an active practice of mine. He asked that I reach for another journal. I handed him one, and he opened up to his son's graduation pictures. He shared stories and memories of his family as well as their achievements. He emphasized the importance of journaling not only dreams, but everyday life as well, because one day, your family would have the story of their lives in their hands.

We flipped to another page in his journal which had additional pictures. He identified an individual in the picture and began speaking about the importance of teaching independence and self-value in handicapped populations. He then shared a story of the great success of the individual in the photo, explaining that this person, like my mom, has disabilities. This brought us to the importance of work–life balance. We exchanged views of harmonizing the two and had a mutual belief that the key to success is happiness with this balance. This elicited an exchange of more personal recollections and stories. Our conversations also brought about the puzzling qualities of life, which touched upon a question I had been wanting to ask Hobson. "Through all of your years of studying and research, and looking and talking about dreams," I began, "what still puzzles you the most about them?" Hobson paused and then shared "The way dreaming informs consciousness. That is on my mind these days. It seems to me that the study of consciousness is extremely problematic, it is very difficult, yet the sleep research is quite easy." This of course, got my gears turning, as we began discussing consciousness, subjectivity, and the ways in which subjectivity can become scientific. "Don't tell this to admissions committees," he said, "they will think you are a kook, and they won't want ya." I will save my social justice plug about the disregard for human experience in scientific inquiry, but this statement definitely caught my attention – and clearly it was on Hobson's mind as well.

The conversation then shifted frames. "And that's another thing," he continued, "I have a piece of advice for younger people. Buy your second home first. Buy something so you have a touchstone." This led us to ambiences of *home* and mutually familiar places with connections we have in common. We spoke of relationships we have to places – birth towns, summer camps, and family members attending universities in specific locations – and then found ourselves making associations to various affiliations we have with people. Hobson spoke of Karl Friston, a neuroscientist who he is currently collaborating with. Hobson then asked about other connections I have in my life. He asked about interviews I have already conducted, and what I have found thus far. I spoke about the significance of relationship surpassing the use of interpretations in dream work. This galvanized the sharing of another of his views. "The interpretive process, it tells you the way the working mind works in relation to the sleeping mind and the more we integrate the two the better," he shared. I followed up with a question of his view of the meaningfulness of dreams. "My dreams are extremely meaningful," he began. "I never said they weren't. People attribute me to the idea that dreams are meaningless, but that's not true. I said from the start that dreaming was meaningful and that dreaming revealed meaning rather than described it."

Our dialogue continued for a long time. We discussed dreams in their relation to family and cerebral dynamics. We deliberated over developing theories of dreaming informed by the latest neuroscience. We spoke of the reflexivity of the mind, the importance of reevaluating previous rigid stances and disavowals, and the value of being taught to use our minds rather than being told information. We even made mention to the interface of gender identity with relationships. Hobson told me about his parents. He spoke of his relationship to his parents, his dreams about his parents, and even shared incredibly moving stories about memorable interactions and relational regrets. We connected over our relationships to our parents and how those relationships manifest in dreams.

Within just an hour and a half, Hobson had taught me about more than just science and dreams. He also taught me about life. When our first hour and a half of talking was up (Hobson had a phone meeting scheduled), it was time for me to visit his dream museum while he spoke on the phone. The museum was in a barn on his property, not even 50 yards from the entrance to his house. The entrance level of the barn looked as though . . . well, it looked as though it was an old barn. But, when I ventured up the stairs towards the main level of the museum, the atmosphere began to change.

At the top of the steps were three rooms. I went into the room on my right first. When I entered, there was a large, finished office. There were wooden bookshelves with glass doors protecting classical texts from authors like Darwin, an abundance of medical encyclopedias and dictionaries, neuroanatomy books, and more. Shelves had labeled pictures of people such as John S. Antrobus and Ken Hugdahl, as well as a signed picture from John Bowlby. The walls were painted with plaques of awards and honors, such as Hobson's Peter C. Farrell Prize in Sleep Medicine from Harvard Medical School. Supplemental to his own awards, the walls bestowed portraits of historical figures including that of neurophysiologist Thomas Graham Brown. Adjacent shelves were full of hundreds of medical and academic journals. Beside his desk stood multiple large, rolled up scrolls which I assumed to be medical posters. Old phrenology statues decorated desk space, and medals of honor accented lamp shades. This was all in just one of three rooms.

The next room I entered looked like an extension of the first. There were additional medical posters and brain images hung on the walls. Like a true museum, each picture was accompanied by a title and written description. Old newspaper articles from *The New York Times* and *Boston Globe* that featured sleep or sleep research were framed and hung. A large round table in the middle of the room displayed additional journals and books. File cabinets held hundreds of writings on various subject matters.

After searching around the second room, I decided to go into the third room. I was in for a big surprise. When I entered, I sat in front of a television which had an introductory video explaining the history of the barn in which the museum was located, as well as the exhibits within the museum. The video ended, and I began to wander around. Directly behind the television viewing area was a portrait that took up an entire wall. It was the *Experimental Portrait of the Sleeping Brain* (Hobson, Spagna, & Earls, 1977). The portrait was composed of a series of miniature snapshots of the different positions an individual assumed while sleeping throughout the night. Adjacent to this portrait were illustrations of the work of neuroanatomist Arnold Scheibel. Across from Scheibel's work was the work of other forerunners in brain research such as neurophysiologist Ruth Bleier. On the opposite side of the television set was a model sleep chamber. The sleep chamber consisted of a bed inside of a glass room with a sleeping mannequin under the covers. Outside of the model chamber were X-rays of a human skull, as well as a human brain preserved in a glass jar. Across from this display spread across a long wall were more television monitors with neuroanatomy images displayed on the screens and framed pictures of what seemed to be excerpts from medical textbooks. The excerpts explained everything from the cell structure and function of the nervous system to REM sleep and theories of dreaming. As I walked down towards the end of the room, I came across a doorway leading into the silo of the barn. The silo, as I would soon find out, had been converted into a four-story library. The staircase was located in the middle of the silo, and as I entered, the cylindrical walls surrounding me were full of files or shelves. The first floor was dedicated to files full of Hobson's personal writings and the writings of others. There were at least eight file cabinets with three drawers each encircling the first floor. Each of the file drawers were filled with over 50 file folders of different writings. I then ventured up to the second and third floors of the silo. Each of these floors was dedicated to shelves full of books. Books were primarily medical and neurological in nature but displayed a multitude of topics. On two of the shelves of either the second or third floor (I cannot quite remember) were at least 15 wooden cases full of brain microscope slides. I was in absolute awe. I then decided to go to the fourth and final floor of the silo. This floor was the lounge. There was a bench following the curves of the cylindrical wall underneath windows providing a 360-degree view of the beautiful, lush green farm land on which Hobson's home is located. It was a reader's paradise.

I sat in the lounge for a couple of minutes, collecting my thoughts of the marvel I had just encountered. After gathering myself and going through the museum a second time to take pictures, a sign that said "Dreamstage" prompted a memory. Prior to my visit, I read a *New York Times* article about the museum. The museum came about from a multimedia exhibition that Hobson took on tour internationally from the late 1970s to the early 1980s. The exhibition was on sleep and dreams and was titled "Dreamstage" (Zezima, 2007). Hobson shared this resource with the public by allowing school field trips to the museum. He eventually worked together with local school teachers to develop a curriculum on sleep and the brain so that children could relate to museum material (Zezima, 2007). I finished taking my pictures and then left the barn, venturing back into Hobson's home to continue our conversation.

When I sat back down in my seat on the opposite side of his desk, he asked for my opinion of the dream museum. I shared my enthusiasm and astonishment. We talked a bit about the museum, its history, and reasons why all of the material was in Hobson's possession. I tried to ask more questions, but I was still in awe and questions would not formulate. Luckily, Hobson is good at conversation, and we found ourselves talking about family again, the nature being access to health care. We conversed over difficulties associated with health insurance and about work I am involved in, which aims to combat access to care issues within the state of New Hampshire. It was at this moment that Hobson said to me, "I told you I believe in people, and I believe in you." This was unexpected, and I was touched. I thanked him, and he began to share his thoughts about the difficulties in facilitating change. We spoke of humans' relationships with interrelation as well as the mind's amazing deceptive abilities that allow people to hide from the truth and avoid change. Hobson shared that he believes part of this leaning has to do with the tendency for humans to compartmentalize and oversimplify things. He reiterated that it is hard for people to admit that things are as complex as they are and feel comfortable about that (our conversation became very meta). "I wonder if this has anything to do with fear of living inside of something we cannot possible conceive of," I asked. "That's partially it, but again, I guess I think we can conceive of it, and we should," Hobson replied.

At this point, Hobson wanted to know more about my project, and he asked if I had gotten a commitment from Domhoff for an interview and I shared that I had. Hobson expressed his appreciation of Domhoff's critical views. Given that Domhoff is located in California, Hobson asked if I had ever been to the state. I then shared a story of going to California with my sisters. This brought us back to family and Italian culture. Through the topic of Italian culture, we discussed food and espresso and then eventually found ourselves in the topic of religion – as Catholicism is big in Italian culture. We talked about our shared view of the separation of church and state, as well as the power associated with religion.

Sometimes, Hobson's curiosity would get the best of him and he would abruptly shift topics. After discussing the separation of church and state, he became curious about my primary mode of transportation (my car), and then we began discussing experiences Hobson has had with his own personal health. (The two conversations were actually related but it is not my place to share how.)

The more we went on, the more we touched upon. We ventured into topics such as my future life goals, both personal and professional, as well as generational differences in work–life balance. We also discussed my views on clinical practice, which are heavily influenced by prominent figures in my training such as my academic advisor, clinical supervisor, and professional seminar instructor. We spoke of my relationships with each of these individuals, and Hobson shared, "Even if they do not tell you, they enjoy working with you. I know they do."

I decided to take his word for it.

Lunch time rolled around, and we engaged in more small talk while we ate. Two of his books were retrieved for me, and he signed the inside cover of each with a different message. Once lunch was over, it was time for me to head back home. I thanked Hobson multiple times before heading out the door, and then watched as he waved goodbye from his window as I pulled away.

Analysis of interview

Anyone who works with dreams knows of J. Allan Hobson's work. He is a prestigious scientist and has dedicated his life to dream and sleep research. Each person that I interviewed for this book mentioned Hobson and had some type of relationship to his work. Conversely, Hobson also either directly or indirectly identified each of them. He mentioned Domhoff multiple times during our discussion, had a picture of Antrobus in his dream museum, and commented on Blechner being an analyst. The dream world is an interrelated, interconnected world. Everyone involved has a relationship to one another in some shape or form. The interesting thing about the relationship people have to Hobson is the ubiquity of disapproval of a theory he presented over 40 years ago (Blechner being a bit of an exception to this. I will speak more of this later).

As we know from recognition theory (Benjamin, 1995), developing a self is heavily dependent on recognition from others. Getting recognized is also how you develop career identity. This is integral to understanding the frequent association of Hobson to his and McCarley's 45-year-old theory (1977). From a relational standpoint, this model was introduced during the formative stages of the careers of Hobson, Domhoff, Antrobus, and Blechner when they were each developing their professional selves. Activation–synthesis theory, however, perturbed all that they knew about dreams and the brain (inadvertently also perturbing the development of their professional selves). Theoretically speaking, Hobson did not *recognize* (Benjamin, 1995) the attempts of the other to contribute to existing knowledge and develop their professional selves, thus facilitating a sense of disintegration due to lack of recognition and loss of self.

In an attempt to connect with the information proposed by Hobson – or, in an attempt to attain recognition – various researchers/academics, and developing professionals, relied on discipline-aligned epistemologies to contend with activation–synthesis theory. Epistemologically determined findings, however, did not align with Hobson's theory (perhaps partially due to his polymath approach to scientific inquiry). When this was presented to Hobson, he felt unrecognized by others, leading him to take a more closed-off and abrasive stance, speaking with certainty as a means of aggressively seeking recognition (as one does when recognition is denied). This response, however, produced a domino effect as others felt unrecognized by Hobson's stance of certainty. As recognition goes, the more certain Hobson became in his stance, the more certain others became in their own stances, leading to critical views of each other fueled by the injury of an all-encompassing lack of recognition. The power of this injury is apparent through the critical views that individuals such as Domhoff and Antrobus hold on Hobson, and a theory he proposed over 40 years ago.

It is also apparent through Hobson's (2015) self-admittedly abrasive approach to acknowledging those with whom he disagrees. The one exception to this circular dance of *who didn't recognize whom* would be Blechner's views on Hobson. While Blechner spoke of disagreements with activation–synthesis theory, he also spoke of an agreement he held with Hobson regarding Freud's view of dreams. My understanding of this is informed by Blechner's occupation of being an interpersonally oriented psychoanalyst/clinician. Blechner works with ruptures for a living, and therefore he has the ability to find the meaning behind a rupture and relate through that meaning, rather than relate through the event itself. His epistemological leaning is to get less caught up in the details as interpersonalists tend to focus more on what is happening than what is concealed. Most importantly, in this difference in views of Hobson is that Blechner agrees that dreams are not about hiding meaning, but about expressing, finding, and creating meaning.

The lack of recognition that Hobson received early on in his career seems to have permeated his interpersonal approach to fellow professionals. As mentioned earlier, a lack of recognition results in a more closed-off stance in which one speaks with more authority and certainty as a means of aggressively seeking the recognition that has been denied. I have noticed this considerably in Hobson's interactions – both through his writings and in our own conversation – particularly as he was attempting to *figure me out*. If Hobson feels as though an individual is contributing to the lack of recognition of his own work with dreams (i.e., contributing the Cartesian split and not considering both the physical and mental as one, or not taking his own data into consideration while presenting new theories), he becomes rigid in his defense of his own theory and disapproving of the other. Interestingly enough, he still maintains a relationship with these people (even if it is not the friendliest). He values argument because argument leads to greater understanding – this is the sign of a true scientist. Recognition, however, also goes a long way with Hobson. If he feels as though he is sitting with someone who will *recognize* him – someone who is willing to learn, consider multiple perspectives, and think first through curiosity, his demeanor changes considerably. This is something I can attest to personally. My interaction with Hobson was rather pleasant, and our conversation was alive and enlivening – it was fun.

Though the response to a lack of recognition may seem situational, it has actually become important throughout Hobson's career. Hobson is a scientist. In the world of science, data that cannot be quantitatively measured is not always valued – and for good reason. What this does, however, is set a value on views that are antithetical to those of a polymath, as Hobson also has an imagination, and the capacity to view events from a number of perspectives. Lucky for Hobson, his intellect allows him to utilize a scientific epistemology at the forefront of all interactions. He is a profoundly critical thinker. This provides him with an avenue to defend any unrecognized work with hard data, while he simultaneously holds onto his appreciation and consideration of the influence of the non-quantifiable on scientific research. (Domhoff spoke of this when he commented on Hobson's denial of data informed by a belief that people are hindered in a sleep lab setting – a testable hypothesis regarding a potential threat to validity.) This search for recognition through identifying with the scientific community came through during our interview as well. During our interview, Hobson suggested that I refrain from telling admissions committees that I view subjectivity as a science because they would think I was a "kook." He affirmed that he did not believe I was a "kook" and then engaged me in an intuitive dialogue regarding subjective experiences. Though there is a need to be recognized (a need held by all humans in order to feel a sense of worth), Hobson does not lose sight of the importance in recognizing others. He sees the person behind the science and understands the influence of humanity on discovery.

All of the examples of relational phenomena provided earlier would not have happened without dreams. Antrobus, Domhoff, Blechner, and Hobson all relate to each other first and foremost through their own relationships to working with dreams. Relationships brought each of them into this line of work. Working with dreams provided them each with a relationship to their own selves as they developed a professional identity. The formative experiences of professionalism through work with dreams provided a basis ripe with the presence and absence of recognition which then influenced the types of relationships developed with others in the field. Finally, work conducted with dreams was shared with others through writings, speeches, international exhibits, and clinical practice, thus creating additional relationships. Without dreams, my relationship with Hobson would be non-existent. My interest in my own dreams led me to research leaders within the field of dream work, and my decision to write this book influenced me to reach out to those within the field. Reaching out to individuals such as Hobson led to scheduled meetings, and meetings led to the development of a relationship. My relationship with Hobson continually grew throughout our conversation. We had dreams as our base and then found ourselves discussing family, memories of the past, plans for the future, culture, values, and more. Throughout the interview, Hobson was more interested in me as a person than the concretized interview questions I had listed for our time together. We both shared an interest of dreams, which set a foundation for recognition, a foundation for relating, and a foundation for working through potential space (Winnicott, 1971/1991) to the *something more* (Stern, Sander, & Tronick, 1998) of interpersonal relating.

Summary

In these last 22 pages, I told *my story* of J. Allan Hobson, a psychiatrist and scientist who has dedicated his life to the study of dreams. I provided an overview of prominent accomplishments, as well as a narration of our time together one early spring day. I offered an overview of topics discussed and a depiction of my first-hand experience of visiting his incredible dream museum. I gave my own analysis of the relationships he has with colleagues in the field and their relationships with him. I included an assessment of my own interaction with Dr. Hobson and shared an account of the influence he has had on those interested in dreams. Most importantly, I illustrated the ways in which dreams were essential to all of the above experiences and crucial in Hobson's ability to see the humanity behind scientific research.

6 Pulling it all together

Shaping lives through the synergistic quality of dreams and relationships

I never cried in therapy, at least up until a certain point in time. In hindsight, I laugh about this because now, sitting in the clinician seat, I encourage my patients to connect with their emotions. But I get it. I was there once – and you bet your bottom that hell could freeze over and I still was not going to cry. I was in a certain phase in my life. It was a time in which development and growth were happening rapidly, and I was changing day by day. Still, it felt weird to emote in front of people, and I had too much to vent about to waste precious minutes on blubbering aimlessly in front of a stranger (even though I had been meeting with this *stranger* weekly for 6 months).

One night before therapy, however, I had an intensely distressing dream. Even though I had a list of other things I wanted to talk about in session, I could not get this dream off of my mind. So, I asked my therapist if we could talk about the dream instead. My therapist agreed, and I began describing the dream contents. I figured after my explanation the conversation would fall flat, and we would be able to move onto the next topic. After all, this was a specified and time-limited therapy. My therapist, however, began asking about the different characters of the dream. He wanted to know more and was really interested in my perceptions of each characters' motives. There was one character in particular I was avoiding talking about – me. My therapist picked up on this rather quickly, and when the time was right asked what *dream me* felt in relation to the other characters. I started sobbing.

A week later, I came into therapy again and went straight into emotional content. I skipped my ranting about the superficial events of the previous week and delved into lurking and relentless emotional states, feeling confident in the ability of the therapeutic relationship to contain (Bion, 1967/1993) these experiences. My connection to my therapist grew, and I felt increasingly confident in his ability to help me with whatever I brought to session. He was no longer a stranger, and neither was I.

Prior to my sharing of the dream, my therapist and I frequently sat in the un-thought known (Bollas, 1987). There was more to be said, and that was a mutually felt experience that we discussed after my dream session, but it was not a *thought* experience. It was a *felt* experience. We were continually sitting in the beta elements (Bion, 1967/1993) of my past, session after session, but the relationship could not withstand the transmission from beta to alpha – the relationship was not there. Then, I brought my dream into session. Suddenly, there was a container for this unthought-known experience to be both expressed and processed. Through discussing the dream, I felt more connected to my therapist than I ever had before. This connection significantly strengthened the therapeutic relationship to the point where I felt comfortable *doing work* in session. None of this, I think, would have happened without dreams.

My dream session was a truly formative experience for me. It put me in contact with the liberating feeling of working through something. It also showed me the strength of feeling supported and cared for. In addition to experiences elicited within myself, it provided me with a guide for provoking this series of events for others. Dreams became a scaffold for building new relationships, and those relationships have become essential in my self-development and relational capacity. As I write this story, I am amazed at the progress I have made since a time long ago, when I would refuse to cry in sessions. I now connect with my emotions readily, and encourage the same for others. I have faith in relational capacities to contain experiences and also have faith in the ability of dreams to facilitate that process. I now frequently discuss dreams in my own practice, and while I always had an interest in the topic, it was not until I experienced the synergy between relationships and dreaming that I was able to use this interest in a way that would shape the lives of others.

Argument summary

Dreams create and maintain relationships. They provide a foundation for relating that in turn serves as an influential event in the lives of others. Antrobus, Domhoff, Blechner, and Hobson, each found themselves in the world of dream work – first and foremost through relationship. Relationships to people such as spouses, colleagues such as William Dement, advisors such as Calvin Hall, teachers assigning summer readings, and a series of professors such as Erica Fromm, Leopold Caligor, and Paul Lippmann, as well as collaborations with people such as Fred Snider and Edward Evarts were all formative in the careers of these four individuals. Careers develop first and foremost through relationship.

Throughout the development of each of their careers, these four men have shaped the lives of others as well. They have contributed significantly to the knowledge available regarding dreams, and this knowledge transmits to various populations. From hard empirical data to theory and real-life examples, publications from Antrobus, Domhoff, Blechner, and Hobson have influenced the lives of the general public, students (my writing this book serving as an example), colleagues, and, in some cases, patients.

The word *men* in the previous paragraph is quite eye-catching. Though men are not the only contributors to the existing knowledge we have on dreams, they are the only people who agreed to speak with me. Women I reached out to in this line of work either did not answer or did not want to be interviewed. The dream world is a highly stigmatized world. The field constantly faces attacks on its legitimacy, and I wonder if power dynamics elicited through gender differentials exacerbate the need to take a more protective and guarded stance in a line of work that already faces negative judgement. There are also relational dynamics that I myself pull for. Losing a prominent male figure in my life to early onset Alzheimer's disease, my grandfather, I would not be surprised if my own dynamics of searching for male figures and role-models were at play here (in fact, Hobson and I spoke about my grandfather during our time together). My therapist was an older male, my good friend whom I mention at the beginning of the book is an older male, and each of the four interviewees in this book is an older male. I am a young woman in my 20s, and each of the four people I interviewed are in their 70s and 80s. They all took caretaking roles in which they gave me advice and were actively involved in helping me with my project. From a relational psychoanalytic perspective, it is easy to see the grandfather–granddaughter transference and counter-transferences that may have been transpiring here (and that I suspect were). As the title of this book suggests, it is not always about your mother.

All of us humans have multiple relationships in our lives. As seen in previous chapters, we have relationships with ourselves, our families, our work, ethnicity, culture, and even the culture of the times. Each of these bonds influences the dynamics of other associations. Throughout this book, we have seen how these connections become inextricable from dreams. Examples include, but are not limited to, happenings in history influencing views on dreams and dreams informing relationships to self, other, and more.

Dreams help meaning-making through relationship. This is seen particularly in psychotherapy, as dreams can help establish, maintain, and stimulate the progress of the relationship for therapeutic purposes. Ultimately, an abundance of relational phenomena transpires through dreams. This was particularly salient while interacting with Antrobus, Domhoff, Blechner, and Hobson. In my interview with Dr. John, S. Antrobus, our dialogue regarding dreams felt forced until I was able to recognize difference, re-orient myself to the

here-and-now of our interpersonal communication, as well as participate in recognition (Benjamin, 1995). While speaking with Dr. G. William
Domhoff, he referred to me by first name throughout our conversation and
spoke endlessly of relationships and their influence on his career. Engaging
with Dr. Mark J. Blechner proved that mutuality in contributions to dream
dialogues enriches conversation. Finally, spending half of a day with Dr. J.
Allan Hobson brought awareness to the complexities in recognition processes (Benjamin, 1995) and how the results of these complexities permeate
all interactions. Spending this time together also highlighted the necessity
of *seeing* the person behind the dream, behind the research, and sitting in
front of you.

Dreams are more than just an image of our mind's eye. Dreams are relationships. They are connections to what is around you, what is behind you,
and what is yet to come. They are facilitating bonds that provide a foundation for formative experiences such as self-development, career development, and progress in psychotherapy. They are the framework for important
moments and life-changing experiences. Most importantly, they are the
synergistic counterpart to the most important part of being human – having
relationships.

References

Antrobus, J. S. (n.d.). *About* [Linkedin page]. Retrieved from www.linkedin.com/in/john-s-antrobus-13841812

Antrobus, J. (1983). REM and NREM sleep reports: Comparison of word frequencies by cognitive classes. *Psychophysiology, 20*(5), 562–568. doi:10.1111/j.1469-8986.1983.tb03015.x

Ardito, R. B., & Rabellino, D. (2011). Therapeutic alliance and outcome of psychotherapy: Historical excursus, measurements, and prospects for research. *Frontiers in Psychology, 2*, 270. doi:10.3389/fpsyg.2011.00270

Aron, L. (1996). *A meeting of minds: Mutuality in psychoanalysis.* Hillsdale, NJ: The Analytic Press.

Aron, L., & Harris, A. (Eds.). (1993). *The legacy of Sándor Ferenczi.* Hillsdale, NJ: The Analytic Press, Inc.

Aserinsky, E., & Kleitman, N. (1953). Regularly occurring periods of eye motility and concomitant phenomena, during sleep. *Science, 118*(3062), 273–274. doi:10.1126/science.118.3062.273

Barsness, R. E. (Ed.). (2018). *Core competencies of relational psychoanalysis: A guide to practice, study, and research.* New York, NY: Routledge.

Benjamin, J. (1995). *Like subjects, love objects.* New Haven, CT: Yale University Press.

Benjamin, J. (2004). Beyond doer and done to: An intersubjective view of thirdness. *Psychoanalytic Quarterly, 73*(1), 5–46. doi:10.1002/j.2167-4086.2004.tb00151.x

Benjamin, J. (2010). Where's the gap and what's the difference? The relational view of intersubjectivity, multiple selves and enactments. *Contemporary Psychoanalysis, 46*(1), 112–119. doi:10.1080/00107530.2010.10746042

Benjamin, J. (2017). *Beyond does and done to: Recognition theory, intersubjectivity, and the third.* London, England: Routledge.

Bion, W. R. (1993). *Second thoughts: Selected papers on psycho-analysis.* Northvale, NJ: Jason Aronson, Inc. (Original work published in 1967).

Blechner, M. J. (1983). Changes in the dreams of borderline patients. *Contemporary Psychoanalysis, 19*(3), 485–498. doi:10.1080/00107530.1983.10746621

Blechner, M. J. (1992). Working in the countertransference. *The International Journal of Relational Perspectives, 2*(2), 161–179. doi:10.1080/10481889209538926

Blechner, M. J. (2001). *The dream frontier.* Hillsdale, NJ: The Analytic Press, Inc.

Blechner, M. J. (2018). *The mindbrain and dreams: An exploration of dreaming, thinking and artistic creation.* New York, NY: Routledge

Blechner, M. J. (2020). *Mark J. Blechner, PhD.* Retrieved from www.markblechner.com

Bollas, C. (1987). *The shadow of the object: Psychoanalysis of the unthought known.* New York, NY: Columbia University Press.

Brink, S. G., & Allan, J. A. B. (1992). Dreams of anorexic and bulimic women. *Journal of Analytical Psychology, 37*(3), 275–297. doi:10.1111/j.1465-5922.1992.00275.x

Bromberg, P. M. (2008a). "Mentalize this!": Dissociation, enactment, and clinical process. In E. Jurist, A., Slade, & S. Bergner (Eds.), *Mind to mind: Infant research, neuroscience, and psychoanalysis* (pp. 414–434). New York, NY: Other Press.

Bromberg, P. M. (2008b). Shrinking the tsunami: Affect regulation, dissociation, and the shadow of the flood. *Contemporary Psychoanalysis, 44*(3), 329–350. doi:10.1 080/00107530.2008.10745961

Bromberg, P. M. (2012). Stumbling along and hanging in: If this be technique, make the most of it! *Psychoanalytic Inquiry, 32*(1), 3–17. doi:10.1080/073516 90.2011.553161

Cartwright, R. D., Tipton, L. W., & Wicklund, J. (1980). Focusing on dreams: A preparation program for psychotherapy. *Archives of General Psychiatry, 37*(3), 275–277. doi:10.1001/archpsyc.1980.01780160045004

Dement, W., & Wolpert, E. A. (1958). The relation of eye movements, body motility, and external stimuli to dream content. *Journal of Experimental Psychology, 55*(6), 543–53. doi:10.1037/h0040031

Diemer, R. A., Leslie, K., Vivino, B. L., & Hill, C. E. (1996). Comparison of dream interpretation, event interpretation, and unstructured sessions in brief therapy. *Journal of Counseling Psychology, 43*(1), 99–112. doi:10.1037/0022-0167.43.1.99

Domhoff, G. W. (1969). *A quantitative study of dream content using an objective indicator of dreaming* (Unpublished doctoral dissertation). University of Miami, FL.

Domhoff, G. W. (1985). *The mystique of dreaming: The search for utopia through senoi dream theory.* Los Angeles, CA: University of California Press, Ltd.

Domhoff, G. W. (1996). *Finding meaning in dreams.* New York, NY: Springer Science+Business Media, LLC.

Domhoff, G. W. (2002). *The scientific study of dreams: Neural networks, cognitive development and content analysis.* Washington, DC: American Psychological Association.

Domhoff, G. W. (2018). *The emergence of dreaming.* New York, NY: Oxford University Press.

Domhoff, G. W., & Fox, K. R. C. (2015). Dreaming and the default network: A review, synthesis, and counterintuitive research proposal. *Consciousness and Cognition, 33*, 342–353. doi:10.1016/j.concog.2015.01.019

Domhoff, G. W., & Kamiya, J. (1964). Problems in dream content study with objective indicators: I. A comparison of home and laboratory dream reports. *Archives of General Psychiatry, 11*(5), 519–524. doi:10.1001/archpsyc.1964. 01720290067008

Foulkes, D. (1982). *Children's dreams: Longitudinal studies.* Hoboken, NJ: Wiley Publishing Company.

Foulkes, D., Hollifield, M., Sullivan, B., Bradley, L., & Terry, R. (1990). REM dreaming and cognitive skills at ages 5–8: A cross-sectional study. *International Journal of Behavioral Development, 13*(4), 447–465. doi:10.1177/016502549001300404

Freud, S. (2010). *The interpretation of dreams: The complete and definitive text* (J. Strachey, Ed. & Trans.). New York, NY: Basic Books (Original work published 1900).

Freud, S. (2019). *Introductory lectures on psychoanalysis* (Hall, G. S, Trans.). Boston, MA: Digireads.com (Original work published 1917).

Gordon, L., Gordon, C. (Producers), & Robinson, P. A. (Director). (1989). *Field of dreams* [Motion picture]. United States: Universal Pictures.

Hill, C. E., Diemer, R., Hess, S., Hillyer, A., & Seeman, R. (1993). Are the effects of dream interpretation on session quality, insight, and emotions due to the dream itself, to projection, or to the interpretation process? *Dreaming, 3*(4) 269–280. doi:10.1037/h0094385

Hill, C. E., Geslo, C. J., Gerstenblith, J., Chui, H., Pudasaini, S., Burgard, J., . . . Huang, T. (2013). The dreamscape of psychodynamic psychotherapy: Dreams, dreamers, dream work, consequences, and case studies. *Dreaming, 23*(1), 1–45. doi:10.1037/a0032207

Hill, C. E., Zack, J. S., Wonnell, T. L., Hoffman, M. A., Rochlen, A. B., Goldberg, J. L., . . . Hess, S. (2000). Structured brief therapy with a focus on dreams or loss for clients with troubling dreams and recent loss. *Journal of Counseling Psychology, 47*(1), 90–101. doi:10.1037/0022-0167.47.1.90

Hobson, A. (2015). *Psychodynamic neurology: Dreams, consciousness, and virtual reality.* Boca Raton, FL: CRC Press.

Hobson, J. A., & McCarley, R. W. (1977). The brain as a dream state generator: An activation-synthesis hypothesis of the dream process. *American Journal of Psychiatry, 134*(12), 1335–1348. doi:10.1176/ajp.134.12.1335

Hobson, J. A., Spagna, T., & Earls, P. (1977). *An experimental portrait of the sleeping brain* (portrait). Boston, MA: Carpenter Center for the Visual Arts Harvard University.

Kivlighan, D. M., Hill, C. E., Gelso, C. J., & Baumann, E. (2016). Working alliance, real relationship, session quality, and client improvement in psychodynamic psychotherapy: A longitudinal actor partner interdependence model. *Journal of Counseling Psychology, 63*(2), 149–161. doi:10.1037/COU0000134

Lippmann, P. (2000). *Nocturnes: On listening to dreams.* Hillsdale, NJ: The Analytic Press.

Mahoney, M. J. (1991). *Human change process: The scientific foundations of psychotherapy.* New York, NY: Basic Books, Inc.

Mikulincer, M., Shaver, P. R., & Avihou-Kanza, N. (2011). Individual differences in adult attachment are systematically related to dream narratives. *Attachment and Human Development, 13*(2), 105–123. doi:10.1080/14616734.2011.553918

Mitchell, S. A. (1988). *Relational concepts in psychoanalysis: An integration.* Cambridge, MA: Harvard University Press.

Safran, J. D. (2002). Brief relational psychoanalytic treatment. *Psychoanalytic Dialogues, 12*(2), 171–195. doi:10.1080/10481881209348661

Schneider, A., & Domhoff, G. W. (2020). *A biography of G. William Domhoff.* The Quantitative Study of Dreams. Retrieved from www.dreamresearch.net.

Schredl, M., Bohusch, C., Kahl, J., Mader, A., & Somesan, A. (2000). The use of dreams in psychotherapy: A survey of psychotherapists in private practice. *The Journal of Psychotherapy Practice and Research, 9*(2), 81–87. Retrieved from www.ncbi.nlm.nih.gov/pmc/journals/1745/

Sharf, J., Primavera, L. H., & Diener, M. J. (2010). Dropout and therapeutic alliance: A meta-analysis of adult individual psychotherapy. *Psychotherapy: Theory, Research, Practice, Training, 47*(4), 637–645. doi:10.1037/A0021175

Shedler, J. (2010). The efficacy of psychodynamic psychotherapy. *American Psychologist, 65*(2), 98–109. doi:10.1037/a0018378

Solms, M. (1997). *Institute research in behavioral neuroscience. The neuropsychology of dreams: A clinico-anatomical study.* Mahwah, NJ: Lawrence Erlbaum Associates Publishers.

Stern, D. N., Sander, L. W., & Tronick, E. Z. (1998). Non-interpretive mechanisms in psychoanalytic therapy. The 'something more' than interpretation. The Process of Change Study Group. *The International Journal of Psychoanalysis, 79*(5), 903–921. Retrieved from www.pep-web.org/toc.php?journal=ijp

Watson, J. D., & Crick, F. H. C. (1953). Molecular structure of nucleic acids: A structure for deoxyribose nucleic acid. *Nature, 171*, 737–738. doi:10.1038/171737a0

Winnicott, D. W. W. (1991). *Playing and reality.* New York, NY: Routledge (Original work published 1971).

Zezima, K. (2007, September 30). Mysteries of the brain and the science of sleep, brought to life in a barn. *The New York Times.* Retrieved from www.nytimes.com

Index

Printed in the United States
by Baker & Taylor Publisher Services